Freight Broker Business Startup

The Ultimate Beginners Guide on How to Start and Scale Your Own Successful Freight Brokerage Business with A Practical Step-By-Step System

Introduction

The Freight Transport Industry

The freight transport industry deals with the transportation of merchandise goods, commodities, and cargo. This transportation industry is commonly referenced as shipping primarily because the first common form of goods transportation from one state to another was done by sea.
However, this mode of shipping has diversified and led to the inclusion of other modes of transportation that are quite effective.

Modes of Freight Transportation

The different modes of freight transportation include:

Ship

Actual ships do most of the exports and imports across the world. The countries that majorly rely on ships to transport their cargo have a fleet of ships and crew members responsible for that job. The fleet of a ship a country owns is commonly referred to as a merchant marine or the merchant navy. With the growth of the export and import industry, merchant shipping has become the lifeblood of our world's economy, as it carries approximately 90% of the world's trade with over 102,194 commercial ships working in the freight transportation industry.

Air

Air transportation has slowly become a popular means of transportation for the freight industry. Cargo transported by air is placed in specialized cargo aircraft as well as in luggage compartments in passenger aircraft. It is the fastest, but the most expensive, means of freight transportation.

Ground

Ground or land shipping is done by either a train or truck. It serves the purpose of transporting cargo, merchandise goods, and commodities that arrive through the sea or by air. Transportation companies pick the commodities from the seaport or airport and transport them to their required destination. Ground transportation has made it possible for countries with limited coastlines to never worry about production facilities close to their ports.

Intermodal

The intermodal form refers to the shipment of goods that require more than one type of transportation. This modality primarily uses several shipping containers which are easy to transfer between plane, ship, rail, and truck. Manufacturers use intermodal transportation to deliver goods right at the recipient's door.

How It Works

The freight industry comprises various companies that perform different functions, all with the purpose of delivering cargo right at the recipient's door. The main function of the freight company is to arrange all the essential details required by the cargo transport between the carrier and the shipper.

The freight company will act as an intermediary between carrier and shipper, and this helps in taking off the problems that the two parties would have experienced when working alone. People interested in shipping an item often have a hard time locating good carriers while carriers have a difficult time finding clients. The freight company is able to use its data list, making the search easier for the shipper and gives carriers reliable clients. Once the freight company sets up any shipment, they acquire a commission.

However, a freight company would not be successful were it not for the help of individuals responsible for the success of every shipment made. These individuals are known as freight brokers and freight forwarders. They are responsible for the profit a freight company makes. They also help find shippers and carriers on behalf of the company.

And this book is exactly intended to help you learn about the freight brokerage business and give you the courage to start one. So, let's dive in.

Chapter 1. Who Is the Freight Broker: Difference Between Freight Brokers, Forwarders, and Agents

Who Is a Freight Broker?

A freight broker is a person or business who serves as a go-between between shippers and asset carriers. Freight brokers can also be described as intermediaries between transportation providers and shipping needs.

In order to ensure that the product reaches its final destination, these individuals or corporations merely serve as intermediaries. The freight broker's job is to facilitate the exchange of information between the shipper and the carrier. This guarantees that the cargo is delivered on schedule and in the desired condition.

The safe movement of commodities is not just the responsibility of the person or company in charge of freight transportation. Note that in addition to a freight broker, there are also freight forwarders and freight agents.

What's the difference form a freight forwarder and freight broker? Comparing the two, what are the similarities and differences?

Learning the differences between these three freight businesses makes it easier to identify the responsibilities of a freight broker without mixing up the other responsibilities.

Differences Among a Freight Broker, a Freight Forwarder, and a Freight Agent

The significant differences among a freight broker, a freight forwarder, and a freight agent are in the responsibilities of each party. However, before we dive into the differences of each role, it is essential to note that in the freight transportation business, each of these firms has a substantial impact., as they act as intermediaries. Despite their similarities, each freight intermediary has different technical and legal obligations.

Responsibilities of a Freight Forwarder

A person or a business entity that secures business for various importers and exporters is a freight forwarder. They also have the ability and the facility to:

- Store the cargo belonging to their clients in their warehouses. This is usually done by big forwarding businesses with their own warehouses.
- Arrange forwarding or distribution of cargo, and this is done as per their client's instructions. Delivery of freight could be in various routings or regular routings.
- Negotiate the freight rates. They communicate with shipping lines, and this helps both parties come up with a freight rate that covers their clients' interests.
- Book their clients' cargo with freight transportation as per the client's requirements.
- Prepare landing bills and negotiation/associated shipping documents.
- Issue an approved house bill wherever applicable.
- Sometimes do customs clearance on behalf of their clients.
- May or may not be qualified to ports or customs. If a freight forwarder is not accredited, they are not able to do customs clearance for their customers.

Responsibilities of a Freight Broker

Regardless of whether it is an individual or a company, a freight broker can be responsible for:

- Arranging the transportation of merchandise goods or cargo whether via road, rail, sea, or air on behalf of the freight forwarder, consignee, or shipper.
- Connecting the cargo owner and shipping company. This earns the freight broker a commission.
- Outsourcing all freight transportation activities such as insurance, transport, etc.
- Unlike freight forwarders, freight brokers do not own company landing bills.
- Other responsibilities freight brokers have included the assessment of shipper's credit, paying motor carriers, collecting receivables, and invoicing shippers among others.

Responsibilities of a Freight Agent

Freight agents are responsible for:

- The estimation of postal/freight rates and the recording of shipment weights and costs
- Keeping records of every good shipped, stored, and received.
- Entering the shipping information of a customer's cargo into a computer.

- Checking import and export documents to determine the customer's cargo content. They later use the tariff coding system, and this helps them classify each good accordingly.
- Preparing manifests on behalf of their customers and transmitting that data to the various cargo destinations.

Unlike a freight broker and a freight forwarder, the responsibilities of a freight agent are more customer-focused. Freight agents also work under licensed freight brokers. However, despite the significant differences between these three freight jobs, each company or individual has to work closely together with the other entity to ensure the successful transportation of their client's goods.

A freight brokerage business cannot work independently, and it requires the help of a freight forwarder, as well as the help of a freight agent to run smoothly.

How Does a Freight Brokerage Business Work?

Just like a freight broker, a freight brokerage business's main function is to connect manufacturing companies or shippers with carriers to ensure that goods arrive safely to their destinations. Understanding how the freight brokerage business works will help you understand the relationship between a freight broker, a shipper, and a carrier. Here is a step-by-step process of how the freight brokerage business works.

Order tender: The first step of this process starts when a business (the shipper) emailing or calling a freight broker for pickup. The freight broker then goes ahead and acquires all the necessary information they require when tendering the freight. The info the shipper provides helps the freight broker determine whether the cargo is a special order or a regularly scheduled shipment.

In addition to the shipment information, they also inquire about the delivery location of the freight and the contact information. They also need to know whether the freight has special handling and packaging instructions, the equipment, the freight's compliance standards, and the consignee's preference.

Freight Scheduling: Once the freight broker has obtained the relevant information about the freight, the next step is to enter the freight order into the freight management system. This system enables freight brokers to schedule and confirm the exact date the order needs to be picked up and delivered.

This is the stage where the services of a freight broker are most valuable. They take time to secure the necessary transportation by selling and booking a professional carrier for the order. Freight brokers build networks with vetted carriers, and they end up forming long-lasting relationships with reliable carriers.

The freight scheduling stage is also where the carrier shares important handling information with the freight broker. Before booking a carrier, the freight broker has to confirm whether the carrier has:

- Appropriate equipment that is up to date and clean
- A current and valid license
- The required number of cargo and a liability insurance cover
- Ability to handle special needs like team transit and driver-assist among others
- A trailer that will not carry any potential contaminants
- Commitment to the delivery time

Dispatch: Once the freight scheduling process is complete, the next step is the dispatch stage. When the time finally comes for the freight to be picked up, the freight broker connects with the carrier, double checks all the essential information like the name, cell phone number, trailer type, and the current location of the carrier. The freight broker also recommunicates the handling requirements of the freight and later gives the carrier the pickup information.

Loading: The freight broker stays in touch with the carrier during the entire loading process. The loading process is not
considered complete until the cargo is placed on the trailer. The trailer is then shut or sealed, and then the carrier signs the shipper's Bill of Landing. Signing the bill means that the carrier accepts liability and possession of the freight.

When communicating with the carrier, the freight broker verifies the case count and skid. They also verify whether the carrier is loading the right freight and its destination as shown on the bill.

This step is necessary as it prevents the transportation of the wrong products, and can derail the delivery time of the goods, leading to unnecessary stress to the shipper and the freight broker.

Transit: The freight broker stays in contact with the carrier throughout the transportation process. They use technology like a GPS tracker to track the progress of the cargo and maintain the location of the freight during each stage. Freight brokers also make regular calls to the carriers during the transit stage to ensure that everything stays on track and that the carrier does not miss appointments.

Freight brokers also help carriers with directions when they get lost during the transit of the freight. They also act as liaisons between the world and the carriers since they inform drivers about the hurdles, they may experience ahead of their journeys like weather delays or traffic.

Delivery and unloading: Once a carrier arrives at the specified destination, the driver is required to document the arrival time in case there are any delays at the drop-off site. If a carrier waits beyond a specific time, they end up getting charged for the delays.

Once the carrier offloads the freight, the consignee goes ahead and signs, noting any damages or shortages. Once they sign these documents, they accept possession of the delivered products. The consignee later documents the time the freight arrived and when it was unloaded. The freight broker then waits for the carrier to turn over their paperwork for the shipper to invoice, and the carrier's payments can also be released.

Billing: Once the freight broker receives the carrier's invoice and the necessary paperwork from the shipper, the freight brokers start processing invoices and sending out bills. Some of the vital paperwork freight brokers require to create invoices includes driver work receipts, BOL, rate confirmation, and lumper receipts. These are documents they need to create for the invoice they need to send to the shippers.

Chapter 2. Freight Brokerage Industry Overview

What Is Freight Brokerage?

Freight brokerage is a business that provides shipment services to companies and individuals for goods they are transporting.

Freight brokers are merchants of transportation. They buy transports to fill their wheeled grid with cargo, then match the cargo with shippers who need it transported. Because of the complex nature of matching specific goods with specific transportation companies, freight brokers had been traditionally set-up as small, local operations.

For businesses that need to transport goods around the world, freight brokerage can save money and time while giving them more control over shipment delivery and handling.

Freight Brokerage Industry

The freight brokerage industry has existed for over 100 years. It was started in the late 19th century by small, independent agents in various locations around the world. In recent years, however, consolidation has taken place among these different firms and major national and international freight brokerage companies have emerged. These major freight brokerage companies handle all of their own business operations internally, including transportation, billing, and customer service.

Freight brokerage is a business that provides shipment services to companies and individuals for goods they are transporting. Freight brokers can be licensed or unlicensed depending on which state they operate in within the United States.

Freight brokerage is a business that involves the buying, selling, transporting, and delivery of freight and cargo. It can be a very lucrative industry because freight brokerage companies can find ways to fulfill the needs of their clients' cargo transportation.

The biggest benefit for freight brokers is that they help businesses by finding the best rates for their shipping needs. This is done by assessing all options. The freight brokers may be able to use several carriers depending on the route taken and size of the shipment. The rates that are usually charged are based on volume, weight and distance traveled. Using more than one carrier can often give the freight brokerage company the opportunity to compare rates. When a business has too much cargo that may not fill up a whole truck, freight brokers often use partial loads and go through the process of consolidating cargo with other shipments. A typical contract for transport will be agreed upon by both parties and once all of the details have been worked out, freight brokers will find the best route for the cargo to take, saving their client time and money.

The global market for ocean-freight transportation is huge – of all the commodities shipped around the world each year, over 80% are transported by sea. Within this market, freight brokerage is a fast-growing industry, growing at an average of 5% per year.

Why Use a Freight Broker?

- All businesses and individuals can use a freight broker. The cost of owning and operating a truck, railcar, plane, or boat is significant. If you are not using the asset everyday it costs you money and the opportunity to earn money by doing something else! Using a Freighter gives your business the opportunity to do other things while someone else runs your shipments for you.
- There are thousands of Freight Brokers worldwide and even more carriers. Finding who is available when you need them can be almost impossible.

Chapter 3. Why You Should Become a Freight Broker

The job outlook for a freight broker is promising since it is the fastest-growing occupational category within the transportation industry; 29% compared to other occupations. As the economy improves and online shopping increases in popularity, freight brokers are becoming more in demand than ever before. If you still aren't sure about becoming a freight broker, then consider the following reasons why you should become enter this business.

An Independent Career

If you become a freight broker, you are choosing to become your own boss and call all the shots. You can easily start as a single person and then add employees as you grow. Either way, you don't have to worry about working for a boss anymore, and you can make your own decisions.

More Time for Important Things

Often, a truck driver must be on the road for at least six days a week. Working an office job means being stuck in the 9 to 5, five days a week. All of this takes you away from more important things such as spending time with family and friends or even just taking some time for yourself.
When you're a freight broker, you can set your own work hours. This allows you to give more time to the people you love or simply unwind and do what you want to do. With the smartphones of today, the work of a freight broker has become much easier; you can take your job with you in most cases and enjoy the freedom.

Better Income

As a freight broker you know the industry and you have an industry network worth a lot of money at your disposal. Take advantage of this network access to add services to your freight brokerage such as trucking operations, and you'll not only be growing your business, but also increasing your income, since you won't have others cutting into your revenues.

No Commute

Perhaps the biggest draw for most is the idea of earning a living while working from the comforts of your own home. You can enjoy your lunch and set your own hours. You don't have to get up early only to be stuck in traffic for hours. Plus, you have the option to sleep on occasions. Also, there's no dress code, sounds fun right? Well, it can be.

Low Start-Up Costs

If you have a strong credit, then you are likely to start your freight broker career with less than $5,000. Because you have the freedom to start from scratch and add on to your workspace and coverage as you want. Read on, and you will see how.

Low Overhead Expenses

If you're working by yourself from home, then you'll be saving a lot of money on overhead costs. Most of your time is spent negotiating on the phone with shippers and carriers or on the computer researching and tracking shipments. This all means a freight broker can keep their expenses as low as $400-$500 per month.

Unlimited Earning Potential

The freight industry is booming, and the only limit to your income is how committed you are to success. As e-commerce grows and flourishes, there is plenty of business to be had for new freight brokers.

Growing Business

The more you grow your freight brokerage business, the more you are increasing your position in the industry. This means you are always building new contacts. This leads to a job that has never-ending expansion potential.

A Family Business

If you have a family, then a freight brokerage can be an excellent way to not only provide for the family, but also allow the whole family to get involved. You can start teaching your children about the job and pass it along to them. The possibilities for work your family can do are endless.

A Family Legacy

When you run your freight brokerage right, you can have an asset that takes care of your family for generations to come.
The advantages of working as a freight broker are several, and it's easy to see why. So now that you're probably on the side of getting into this field, let's consider a little more about the industry to get you the knowledge you need to get started.

Chapter 4. How to Become a Freight Broker

A successful freight broker's first and most important step is gaining enough industry experience and knowledge. While a freight brokering business may not require you to have prior experience and knowledge, you can still acquire the knowledge and expertise you need to be the best in this field through diligence and patience. So, how exactly can you gain these things to make it in the freight broker sector?

Development or Refreshment of Some General Skills

The first and most important skill any freight broker should possess is a strong will. This is absolutely necessary as it helps freight brokers make it through, especially when things are not as good as you had hoped in business. Other essential skills you require to develop or refresh as a freight broker include:

Strategy Skills:

Strategy skills are among the most significant skills needed to make you successful as a freight broker. With the various links along the supply chain required for you to safely transport merchandise goods from one place to the next, you need to have the capability to come up with creative strategies that will help you get the job done.
Strategic skills are not inborn, you need to improve them continually, or else your freight brokerage business can become dysfunctional. Deliveries may end up not getting to their destinations on time, and this can cause you to lose your business eventually. Once you learn to hone your strategic skill, you also start succeeding as a freight broker.

Organization Skills:

Starting a freight brokerage business means that you will be in charge of all the work done within your agency. This entails working independently, and it can be quite a challenge for an individual not used to working without assistance. You become your own booker, personal assistant, scheduler, financial planner, and strategist. On top of all these new responsibilities, you have to ensure you manage the daily influx of orders and requests. Without organization skills, it becomes relatively impossible to compete with other freight brokers in the industry. Developing your organizational skills will help set your business apart from other freight brokerage agencies in the industry. Strong organizational skills will enable you to offer your clients high-quality services and remain proactive in the industry.

Communication Skills:

Communication skills are also essential primarily because being a freight broker requires you to communicate regularly with your clients either via email or over the phone. Your communication skills can either make or break your customer relationships. You also require communication skills to negotiate and close deals.
Refreshing your communication skills enables you to stay ahead of your competitors since you can properly relate with your clients and this allows you to offer them quality services.

People Skills:

People skills in the freight broker industry go beyond treating your employees with respect and helping your clients. It involves your ability to connect with your clients and vendors. If your daily interactions with vendors and clients are fraught with misunderstandings and tension, then there is a big problem with your communication skills.
A freight broker with exceptional people skills has the ability to express him or herself in an understanding and respectful manner, especially when under pressure. They also make it their primary goal to help their vendors, clients, and customers get the job done no matter the obstacles. People skills do come in handy in helping you maintain your business as it enables you to create long-lasting relationships and networks in the industry.

Management Skills:

Successful freight brokers are excellent managers of every shipping task they are entrusted with by their clients. Any successful freight broker can tell you that it is quite easy to get overwhelmed by the numerous tasks you are required to perform. This is where you put your management skills to work and lighten the workload.
Management skills help you delegate tasks accordingly, that is in case you have employees. But if you are working on your own, you are able to delegate your tasks in a manner that will not overwhelm you. The ability to exercise your management skills requires you to have excellent knowledge about this industry; you should also know your responsibilities, and learn what interpersonal skills you need to become a successful freight broker.

Business Skills:

Every successful freight broker requires a business for them to grow, develop, and increase their earnings. You will need to build your business, and this will need some business skills, and they include:

- Financial planning: helps you design strategies in advance over the long-term, and this keeps your business from failing.

- Negotiating prowess: whether you are negotiating with a client or a national carrier or merely trying to figure out the right commission rate you require; negotiation skills help you maximize profits.
- Marketing knowledge: Thanks to technology, marketing skills have become a necessary tool for individuals to grow their businesses. Having marketing knowledge is quite essential for freight brokers who want to succeed in their businesses.
- Networking skills: Building a list of contacts and clients as a freight broker requires networking skills. As you are building connections, you also have to be strategic with the connections you make. Carefully think about the contacts that can help grow your business both indirectly and directly and then start networking.

Just because you work independently, it does not mean that you do not require other people for you to succeed as a freight broker. In addition, networking with other freight brokerage businesses is also another way for you to unlock the potential your business has by creating smart connections with other businesses.

Multi-Tasking Skills:

Every successful freight broker can tell you that having the ability to handle more than one task is essential in this industry. For instance, the first part of your day could be spent building your clientele while the remaining portion of your day can be spent contacting vendors and processing invoices. At the same time, you could also be in contact with drivers moving the freight.

Balancing all these activities requires you to have multi-tasking skills. However, before you get to the level where you can handle taking on two tasks at once, start small and build up your capacity to tackle more than one responsibility.

Technical Skills:

Thanks to technology, the freight industry has improved tremendously in the quality of services they offer. This means that your ability to compete in the freight broker industry will be dependent on your technical skills. You, therefore, have to be ready to integrate technology into your business, making it more efficient and cost-effective for your clients and you.

You also have to start figuring out ways you can integrate driverless carriers into your business along with other beneficial services.

Compliance Skills:

Every state and city have its own rules for hauling freight. Knowing these regulations may not be part of your job description, but it is essential for you to understand and comply with the rules of different states as a freight broker.
This will help prevent your loads from being stopped during transportation because you did not comply with a particular regulation.

Logistics Planning skills:

Customers look for freight broker services because they require logistics support when transporting their freight. As the freight broker, your customers are counting on you to act as an intermediary between the shippers and carriers and ensure the safe transportation of their freight. This is where logistics planning skills come in handy.
Logistics planning skills help you offer your clients information about the specific routes they can use to transport their freight. You are also able to analyze the information and provide them advice they can use to make the best decisions.

Taking Freight Brokerage Training

Besides having the skills, I have listed above, you also require knowledge about the freight broker industry that you can acquire by attending a freight broker school or taking freight broker courses. These courses help you prepare and learn about the actual requirements and responsibilities of your job as a freight broker.
However, the best option to acquire freight broker training is through attending freight broker classes. Through technology, you can now have access to other freight broker courses; which begs the question, how do you choose the right course among numerous courses?
The first step is through conducting a simple online search, and this will yield numerous results. Next, visit the website of the schools that interest you, look at the cost of the training, the length of time for each course, and the school's program offering.
Some of the schools that offer online programs, which train students to become exceptional freight brokers are California State University (that has a freight broker certificate program), the University of Houston, and the California East Bay State University.

What Can You Learn from Freight Broker Courses?

Freight broker courses enable freight brokers to develop the skills required to take the Federal Motor Carrier Safety Administration (FMCSA) broker's license exam. Though you may not need this license to practice as a freight broker, you require it to start a freight brokerage business.

Investing in freight broker courses is the best way to:

- Study the history of the freight industry and its unique points.
- Learn how to start and operate a freight brokerage company.
- Understand the differences between freight brokers, freight agents, and freight forwarders.
- Get an introduction to record-keeping practices that will enable you to organize your business appropriately.
- Get the basics on how to prepare appropriate documentation for your freight brokerage business; how to contact potential clients; and market your business.
- Obtain a deep insight into how the industry works, as well as its main players
- Acquire practical knowledge about your responsibilities as a freight broker.

Let us not forget that the training you receive from these courses can also open doors of opportunity for your business.

Whatever course you settle for, ensure that it is one that offers sufficient training about the freight industry and an in-depth working of this industry.

Chapter 5. Starting Your Own Freight Brokerage Business: An Easy-To-Follow Road Map

Now that you have all the required knowledge to operate a freight brokerage business, the next move is to apply for a state license to operate your business. You will need to form your own Limited Liability Company or LLC. You need to understand how the process goes so that you can do it yourself with ease. If you find the steps too challenging or complex, then you can hire a lawyer for some advice, preferably the ones who specialize in drafting and setting up businesses. However, we think that the process is pretty simple and straightforward. See the steps below:

Design an Impressive Business Plan

To begin, the most important step you should take probably is outlining an excellent business plan that will see you overcome any possible challenges, beat the competition, and thrive. To be successful, you really have to understand all aspects of the business.

Step-By-Step Procedure in Creating a Business Plan

1. Define the Freight Broker's Business

One should start with the understanding of what a freight broker does. A freight broker is someone who aids businesses in transporting goods by taking care of logistics and arranging the shipment of either products or raw materials.

2. Who Is Your Target Market?

Now, you have to understand who your target market is, so that you can tailor your business plan accordingly and make it more relevant to them. Understanding your company's target market will allow you to choose which industry best suits it, the type of warehouse space needed, as well as which position within the company best fits their career interests, experience level, and financial needs.

3. Research the Industry of Freight Broker

As part of the business plan, you must research the industry that you are creating; understand its structure, as well as how a freight broker fits into it. Freight brokers are generally classified according to their mode of operation. A freight broker is classified as either a company which transports goods personally, on behalf of its customers, or an individual who transports goods himself or herself, also known as an owner-operator. The number and size of all types of freight brokers will be different in different parts of the country with large metropolitan areas, usually providing more opportunities for advancement than rural areas.

4. Financial Projections

Before entering into a business, one should have a fairly good idea of how much money is needed to run it, and the operating costs. One should also be aware of the profit margin likely to be made from this business. The best way to gather information about operating costs would be to speak with those who are already in this business and have some experience.

5. Market Research

After the financial projections have been made, market research should be done. This should include input from potential customers and competitors. Those in charge of marketing the goods for sale can assist with understanding the current and future needs of their customers.

6. Plan for Legal Structure

One should then plan for a legal structure that best suits our business operations such as a limited liability corporation, partnership, or sole proprietorship. These steps would require consulting an attorney who will be able to guide you through this process and ensure that you have all appropriate documents in place before the operation begins.

7. Work on Management

Once the legal structure of the business is in place, one should then focus on management. The types of employees that may be needed for this business include a sales staff and various types of warehouse workers, including stock people, inventory managers, material handlers, and drivers. One should also plan to hire a bookkeeper to keep up with accounting records and payroll for employees.

8. Market the Business

One should then begin marketing the freight broker business by developing a logo for the company, which will be used on all materials related operations. Likewise, you must come up with a name that represents the company well according to target markets. Business cards and brochures should also be designed. The marketing of a freight broker will be based on the number of sales it can make within a given time period. Those who have excellent sales skills will do well as freight brokers in this industry.

9. Implement Sales Strategies

Each type of freight broker uses different sales strategies, so having an idea of how your competitors operate their business would be very useful in coming up with an effective plan to sell your services within that industry.

10. Purchase Equipment

As part of the company startup process, one should purchase the equipment needed to run the freight broker business, including office furniture, computer hardware, software, and bookkeeping software.

11. Write a Business Plan

The final step in creating a business plan for a freight broker is to write it down. One should start by writing an executive summary, which will include a written description of the target market, along with information about how the business began, such as how much money was raised to launch it; why you decided to launch the business; and what are the goals and objectives for its operation.

Identify a Suitable Business Name That Conforms to the State's Business Registration Rules

Prepare your paperwork by filling out all the necessary forms and providing all the required information, including personal details and contact information.
Once the paperwork is ready, submit it all together with all required attachments.
Accompany the paperwork with the required fees. The fees can range anywhere from $100-$800 depending on the rules and your state.

Now come up with a suitable LLC operating agreement whose role is to indicate the rights and responsibilities of LLC members. Once these are published, you then need to publish a notice of intent that lets the general public known that you wish to form an LLC. Follow this procedure only if it is a requirement in your state.

After your business is registered, you can then proceed to apply for other licenses and permits necessary for operations.

The Business Registration Process

The process of registering your business begins at the office of the Secretary of State within your state. The registration procedures will vary from state to state. However, the process generally begins with your secretary of state's office.

Sometimes you may be required to head over to the local tax office at the Department of Revenue to register as a taxpayer. Business tax registration is crucial if you are to operate legally, as required. When registering your business, you will not be limited only to a Limited Liability Company. There are other options available as well. They include the following:

- Partnership.
- Sole proprietorship.
- Corporation.

As you choose the best fit for your business, remember that there is no wrong or right choice. What matters is identifying the most suitable form of business that you require.

Learn about Truck Load Boards

Load board or freight board is a matching system online that lets freight brokers and shippers post loads. The boards also provide for transporters or carriers to post any free equipment in their possession. This makes it convenient for carriers and shippers to find each other and then draft agreements that enable them to work together to move cargo. Many of these load boards are sophisticated platforms. They allow users, shippers, brokers, and transporters, to search or post loads using a particular criterion. The load boards also provide additional services to carriers and freight brokers. Some of these additional services include the following:

- Message boards.
- FMCSA verification.
- Load Matching.
- Financing of pre-approved loads.
- Capacity to note info on shippers and carriers.
- Mobile access.

- The necessary credit information.

You can find a number of load or freight boards out there. Some charge fees, while others are free. The paid ones can be quite costly. You can expect to pay about $100 per month to gain access. Keep in mind that you get exactly what you pay for.
Just remember that paid load boards are not always the best, so Keep looking until you discover the right one for your business.
While load boards are useful, they do have their pros and cons. For instance, if you are a new operator, you are likely to find lots of great opportunities on the board. However, the problem is that they have too many players, and this tends to reduce margins and increase competition to unhealthy levels.

Factoring Invoices Through the Load Board

Many load boards integrate loads together with firms that provide freight bill factoring. The integration enables freight brokers to take on slow-paying freights, so it is a useful feature when you are running low on funds. You get access to crucial financing that can help you pay for any repairs, fuel, and driver. You can also use the funds to take additional loads to expand your operations.
As a truck broker, you will often find that freight bills take pretty long to get settled. Sometimes, even more than sixty days. In such instances, you may require finances to meet your regular or recurrent expenditure. This is where bill factoring comes in handy. It allows you to gain access to much-needed funds, which you can use as you see fit. You can easily factor invoices through a load board. Here is how it is done:
Freight Bill Factoring Process

- Deliver a consignment to your client.
- Then take care of sending a copy of the invoice to the funder and the client.
- Once these are received, the advanced funds will be wired to you.
- The transaction will then be completed once your client pays.

What Are the Benefits of Bill Factoring?

- You enjoy predictable funds access.
- Approvals are often quite fast.
- You have access to pay drivers, repairs, and fuels.
- Sometimes it comes with fuel cards.

Always ensure that you choose the correct factoring company to partner with. You should research how long it will take them to send you funds to finance your initial freight bill. All these are crucial when seeking a funding firm to engage with.

Negotiate the Best Terms

You should be able to engage the company and enter into negotiations to receive the very best terms. The profit margins in the transport sector are minimal, so it is difficult to find wiggle room. The margins are tight, mainly due to stiff competition in the industry. Therefore, the costs will depend on:

- Your shippers and agents' credit.
- Extra or additional fees.
- Factoring rate.
- Factoring advance.

Once your business running, you should ensure that you acquire the correct software. Good quality software can make a huge difference to your business. For instance, quality Transport Management Software (TMS) can help you manage your records and paperwork, plan routes appropriately, dispatch drivers, send invoices, and even set up shipping well in advance. Should a crisis arise, then you can use the tools provided to sort it out.

You will be required to be online most of the time. Truck or freight brokering is as much about computers and the Internet as it is about consignments and deliveries. Online platforms, such as the modern ones that you will be using, are competing seriously with the traditional phone and fax machines. Today, there are apps on the internet that you can use to help manage your business and increase efficiency. Unfortunately, some apps in the market are trying to eliminate brokers from the equation and trying to link consigners or shippers with transporters. Try and find shippers who use standardized shipments that require standard trucks. Sometimes you will need to get into direct contact with firms that provide specialized shipping.

Setting Up Your Freight Brokerage Business

After completing most of the necessary steps, you're ready to get to work. Developing a reputation for yourself is a critical step to take. As a newcomer, no truck company or client will touch you with a ten-foot pole unless you can prove that you have the necessary authority as well as surety bonds. It is only after you are properly registered, licensed, and possess all the essential authority to operate as a freight broker that you begin getting clients and loads.

You will also need to get your finances in order. Many truckers are wary of freight brokers who dish out jobs but do not have the finances to pay for the service.

It is also important if you feel the need to start off as an agent. An agent is basically one who works for an established broker. You can be in a different location with your own office, but the experience is invaluable. Once you receive sufficient experience as an agent, you can then set yourself up as a freight broker. This also provides an excellent way of acquiring your own clients.

It is advisable to expect to hurt and lose money in the first year of business. Unless you are really good or have sufficient experience, a lot of new freight brokers barely break even in the first year. However, if you hang in there, you should start enjoying success. You should expect to foot your costs and expenses for a while, so be prepared for that.

Legal Process Agents

Once your business picks up and you want to set up offices in another state, then you should get an agent. You will require an agent in each state to represent you there. Officially, they are referred to as legal process agents. Legal process agents must be registered in each state where they work. Agents are often registered with the federal government transport department through the FMCSA. You will fill out and submit form number BOC-3. For each form BOC-3 you submit you will be charged a processing fee of approximately $50

Chapter 6. 7 Tips to Avoid the Most Common Pitfalls

It's not an exaggeration to say that avoiding these seven mistakes will put you ahead of most of the freight brokers out there, including the most experienced ones.

Mistake #1: Not Embracing Technology

The freight brokerage industry started in the late 80s and blossomed in the 90s. There's something else that grew during that era—you might have heard of it. It's this thing called the Internet. Smart businesses, including freight brokers, embraced technology wholeheartedly. Some older freight brokers resolutely clung onto the old, manual ways of doing things.

This suited them fine until this decade, where technology has leaped so far forward that it's impossible for the laggards to catch up. This is why I mentioned that avoiding some of these mistakes will put you ahead of some of the most experienced freight brokers in the business. Technology can shortcut your processes and allow you to automate dead tasks. In turn, you can focus more on marketing and the important stuff in your business that actually brings in money.

Installing processes goes beyond embracing tech, though; it's about defining clear workflows because you want employees to always know what you expect of them. Many business owners make the mistake of thinking that their employees are just as capable of handling unstable situations as they are. This isn't always the case, however. You might have had to figure out how to do things from scratch, but expecting your employees to do the same and reinvent the wheel is only going to waste time.

Instead, use technology to automate most tasks that are unimportant, and prepare good documentation that tells your employees exactly what to do when various situations arise. They can then build on those processes and create better ones. Coming back to technology, there are various software programs out there that successful freight brokers utilize.

At a basic level, you need software to handle bookkeeping and accounting. This is a must-have for businesses of all sizes. Don't make the mistake of saving paper receipts and filing them into a spreadsheet yourself. Invest in a high-quality software program, and you'll undoubtedly reap the benefits down the road. Software specific to freight brokering includes transportation management software or TMS.

TMS has been the defining line between success and failure in this industry. The companies that have embraced it have been able to generate huge customer demand and have managed to serve their suppliers with greater traffic, which in turn drives download rates thanks to volume discounts. Many first-time freight brokers think they can bootstrap it and use old-fashioned boards to coordinate freight. This is a bit like turning up to a horse race on a cow. Don't do it.

Business owners often use a lack of capital as justification for the lack of technology in their business. This brings me nicely to the second mistake.

Mistake #2: Not Enough Capital

If there is one mistake you should avoid making when starting out as a freight broker, it's this one. Always be certain you have cash in the bank and that you're adequately capitalized. If you're not, you're headed into a world of pain where every business decision you make is going to be like pulling teeth. Imagine having to decide between food or water in your personal life because you have money for just one expense.

That sounds ridiculous, perhaps, but many business owners force themselves and their businesses into this situation by being naive. Thankfully, you're not naive, because you're reading this book and educating yourself. However, under-capitalization puts even the most promising of businesses out of work.

Most business owners seek to save as much money as possible when starting out. This is natural since cash flow is low and costs are high. However, there's a difference between keeping costs low and shooting yourself in the foot. You should bootstrap your operations as much as possible but not to the extent that you can't afford to buy the tools you need to succeed.

This is why many beginner freight shippers fail—because they think that by doing everything manually, they're keeping costs low. However, they're placing themselves in a position from which they can never compete. So, it doesn't matter how low their costs are as they're never going to succeed. If you can't make money regularly, the amount of expenses you incur is irrelevant. You only succeed when you make a profit.

The profit equation has two parts to it: costs and revenues. Many companies focus solely on costs and think revenues will take care of themselves. However, you need to actively invest money to generate revenues. Note that I used the word invest, not spend. Investing money to buy software is not an expenditure; it's something that will pay you back many multiples over in utility.

Similarly, hiring great employees who will make money for you and paying them high salaries isn't an expense but an investment. Allocating capital must be your main objective as a business owner.

Your employees will be able to run the day-to-day operations of the company. However, they can do this efficiently only if you provide them with all the resources, they need to do a good job. If you don't do this, it's a bit like buying a fancy sports car and then refusing to fill the tank with premium fuel or avoiding buying good tires that will last for a long time.

Another mistake that occurs due to beginners not being able to distinguish between investment versus expenses is that they go into business without any money. They think bootstrapping equals going into business without any cash, but this isn't so. To make money, you must spend money. This isn't to say that the person who spends the most will earn the most. Instead, understand that the person who invests the most will reap the greatest rewards.

So, look at money and your capital as an investment. It's a resource. Where will you put it to work? Put it into something that won't generate a return so you lose money. Put it into something that will grow over time so you make money. Creating processes, buying software, and hiring good employees are all examples of investments that will benefit your business.

Money powers investment. So, read this book carefully to see how much you need to start your business and do it the right way.

Mistake #3: Inept Procedures and Processes

I've briefly mentioned the importance of processes thus far, but it's worth taking the time to dive deeply into how important procedures and processes are for your business. A process is what differentiates a one-person shop from a large company. When you employ even one person, you'll be tasked with helping them do their job well. Not only do they need to do their job effectively, but in addition, they must provide a profit for you that exceeds the amount you paid for them.

There's no technology that exists yet that allows people to transfer their thoughts directly to another person, nor is your employee likely to be a mind reader. The only way you can assist them out is to create as many standardized processes and procedures, structuring them so that they can be repeated over and over again.

Let's use a simple example. Freight brokers need to regularly hire vet truckers. These people are the suppliers of your business effectively, so they have to be reliable and of high quality. The easiest way to vet them is to create a standard process that every trucker must pass.

For now, I just want to highlight that you as an individual could figure out how to vet a carrier through "feel". However, if you're wanting to grow your business, you need your employee to be able to do this properly. Their "feel" is going to be different from yours. Now let's say you employ 20 people. How can you expect your truckers to be of uniformly high quality if every one of them is going to evaluate truckers based on their own "feel"?

You'll never deliver consistent performance for your customers. This will hit your bottom line. There's a reason I've chosen to highlight trucker vetting procedures. Not vetting carriers and truckers, and choosing to simply work with someone who quotes the lowest price is a surefire recipe for disaster.

There are other processes you need to utilize as well. One of the most important is the employee evaluation process. Who will you hire, and what will you look for in them? How will you identify great people who can take your business higher? Installing a process is the only way to get the answers you want.

Many beginners to the freight brokerage business think that it's all about connecting customers to truckers, and to some extent, this is correct. However, the majority of your time as a business owner will be spent refining and tuning your processes so that everything runs smoothly. If you don't do this, you'll spend all of your time putting out fires. So, focus on building highly repeatable processes that even a novice to the job would understand; don't leave any loose ends; and document everything. This is what will help you build your business.

Mistake #4: Narrow Book of Business

A freight broker's book of business is their customer base. Your customers are shippers and other entities that need goods transported. One of the biggest mistakes that failed freight brokers make is that they relax once they collect a few solid customer contacts. They begin to rely on these customers and expose themselves to failure. After all, if one customer goes down the drain, then the broker's business will also suffer.

This mistake occurs because these business owners don't see marketing as being a constant activity that is as important as operations. Without marketing, there won't be any operations. In fact, when it comes to freight brokering, marketing is more important than operations, because your clients are constantly on the hunt for brokers who can provide them with lower fees.

Your competitors will always be trying to lure your clients away from you. Providing great service is an excellent way of keeping them on board with you, but this doesn't insulate you from the customer's business failing. You need to constantly advertise yourself and install robust marketing processes that will keep your business at the top of every customer's mind. Many freight brokers new to the business are surprised at how fluid their book of business can be. It takes time to develop customer loyalty. When you begin, you'll have to deal with a good amount of turnover, thanks to other brokers luring customers away from you. This also explains why many business owners relax once they've built some degree of customer loyalty. However, relaxing isn't the way to go when you're running a business.

You have to prioritize marketing and positioning yourself as a reliable broker. You'll have a complete marketing plan ready to implement once you're done with it. However, understand that even the best marketing plans need commitment and desire from you. If you're not willing to market yourself with the same degree of energy that you afford to your operations, then you're going to have a tough time of it.

Mistake #5: Dead Invoices

Dead invoices are a common problem in the freight brokerage world. Your customers will pay you, on average, after 60 days while your suppliers will want payment within 30. This creates a cash-flow gap. If your book of business is strong, you can overcome this hurdle pretty easily. However, new businesses rarely have huge customer books that they can lean on.

Leaning on capital reserves or borrowing money remains the only real alternative to overcome this obstacle. Whichever option you choose, you'll have to make collecting outstanding invoices a priority. Too many brokers are afraid of collecting money because they believe their customers will simply desert them. It's true that customers are looking for the longest credit terms possible, but this hardly means you should put yourself in a hole for their sake.

In fact, most customers will treat you according to your expectations. If you don't communicate your terms and payment process clearly, they'll likely take advantage of you and delay payment. Combine this situation with a narrow book of business, and you have a recipe for disaster.

Your processes are what will save you. Automating the monitoring and collection of invoices makes the most sense. Automation costs money, but you're unlikely to miss payments due to poor cash reconciliation to invoices or lose a dispute with a customer because you couldn't pull a record up in time. It goes back to how much you're willing to invest. Most business owners don't consider invoice and payment collection as being worthy areas of investment, instead assuming that it's automatic once the job is done.

However, you have to constantly negotiate credit cycles and work to maximize your cash flow. Letting your invoices sit around collecting dust is a definite way to never get paid. The key is to create processes that allow you to collect payment efficiently and follow up with your customers on time. Dispute handling should also have processes surrounding it so that your employees can quickly track and resolve disputes.

Assist your consumers in paying you by making it as simple as feasible and you'll manage to reduce the cash flow disparity in your business.

Mistake #6: Load Board Dependency

You're going to learn about load boards in great detail later in this book. For now, just understand that a load board is an online system where you can find both customers and truckers. It's a marketplace of sorts where everyone comes together and connects with each other. Many freight brokers base their entire business off of load boards, and this is precisely why so many of them fail.

On some level, it's understandable why this happens. Load boards can have a ton of inquiries and customer requirements. A beginner is apt to think that a good load board presence is all they need to generate steady sales and loads. However, the competition is excessive on these boards because everyone else has had the same idea. As a result, margins are razor-thin, and in some cases, once you add the cost of your time spent on the board, you'll realize you've lost money.

The best freight brokers maintain relationships with their truckers and customers all the time. They grab a hold of loads before the requirement ever gets close to a load board. Here's a little secret: Experienced operators in the business, no matter what their function is, dislike going anywhere near a load board. They know the competition is fierce and the likelihood of them getting their needs fulfilled isn't great. They might find someone to fulfill their requirement, but it's unlikely they'll find it at the price they want.

This is why both customers and truckers rely on freight brokers. No one likes to lose time looking for things on their own. They want the convenience of picking up the phone and connecting with someone who can instantly fulfill their requirements. Freight brokers do this by maintaining great relationships that preempt any need to go to a load board.

So beware of relying solely on a load board, that would be a mistake. Feel free to go to it every now and then to cover a few gaps in your cash flow, but never make it your primary source of revenue.

Mistake #7: Focusing Solely on the Money

You're in business to make money, so it's natural that you'll be focused on the monetary terms of every load that comes by you. However, there are many too-good-to-be-true loads that you will run into. It could be a high revenue load or a low-cost trucker. Many beginners jump into these deals without thinking twice about the implications of what they're signing up for. In our company (and in business in general), there are no free meals, and there's always a catch with such loads.

Perhaps the load could contain cargo that is less than legal or perhaps the insurance does not cover the whole cost of shipping. There are fraudulent truckers who will try to scam you by asking you to wire them money in advance as well. Beware of such offers; there's usually nothing but a painful lesson behind them. Always focus on the terms of the load and on the job that needs to be done.

Excessive focus on money also leads many unsuccessful brokers to destroy the relationships they have in the business. Trust me when I say this: Word gets around. If you don't treat your partners with respect, you're going to be earmarked as someone who isn't reliable. The good-quality truckers and customers will desert you, and you'll have to deal with companies that take 90 days to pay you 50% of your invoice or with truckers who manage to lose your load every single time.

Focus on relationships at all times while keeping the monetary terms feasible for every party. You might have to sacrifice a few points in margin every now and then, but this doesn't mean you should hobble yourself to make it in this business. Everyone you deal with will drive a hard bargain, but that's just a part of doing business. The best deals are win-win for everyone involved. That's what keeps people coming back to you. So, focus on the value you can provide people with, and you'll have no problems making money.

Chapter 7. Start a Home-Based Freight Broker Business or Setting Up an Office

Setting Up Your Home Office

A home office is a good place to begin your career as a freight broker. Not all businesses can be started from home; however, a freight brokerage firm can operate successfully from a home office. Many successful firms today started in basements and living rooms.

Setting up a home office is simple. You'll have to pick a specific space in your house for this project. You need to ensure that this room is set aside from the rest of the house, especially when you are working. For instance, you need to keep the kids away when you are working as well as pets, or even guests.

Adopt a disciplined and official attitude when working, so that others can let you work. No client wants to hear kids playing, dogs barking, or loud music when discussing business.

Essential Home Office Equipment

You will require specific equipment for your home office. If you already have basic pieces of furniture, such as an office desk and a comfortable, sturdy seat, then you are ready to get started.

1. Workstation

You will need a workstation in your home office. This is where you will primarily be working from. Get a large enough table or office desk as well as a high-back chair. If you already have them at home, you can use these as they will save you from buying new ones.

If you do not have an office desk and a high-back chair, then you can easily find these being sold locally or online. You do not have to purchase the most expensive items on the market. Simply find a good quality, functional desk and chair and set these up as soon as you can.

2. Computer, Telephone, and Internet

You will spend most of your working time on your workstation talking on the phone and using your computer. Therefore, get a dedicated office line instead of using the home phone line. This will set aside your private life from your work. It will not appear prudent for a client to call you only to speak to a family member.

Get a nice, modern, fast, and reliable computer for your work. A good computer must be fast, with a large memory capacity, and can handle heavy software programs and the various apps that you will need for your work.

Clear the Clutter

Make sure that your home office is devoid of any clutter: knickknacks, old magazines, newspapers, and even electronics should be removed. These can easily cause a distraction and look unsightly. A cluttered space usually brings about a cluttered mind. However, if you have any items in mind that will motivate and inspire you, then you can add these to your office.

You should strive to be as orderly as possible and stay that way. If you are organized, then you will be productive, creative, and efficient. However, if you are not organized, then you will be counterproductive and distracted. Distraction often comes from things such as incomplete tasks, loose papers, clutter, and so on.

To be organized, you should get a trash can, filing cabinet, and even a shredder for the office. These are simple items but will go a long way in getting you organized so that you are efficient in your work and can focus on delivering quality services to your clients. Some people are messy by nature, and that is easy to understand. If this is you, then it is okay to ask for assistance on how to stay organized.

Set Your Office Hours

While standard office hours are between 9.00 am and 5.00 pm, you may want to experiment with your working hours. Since you are your own boss, then you are allowed to do this. A home-based job offers you the flexibility to choose your preferred time. This way, you can create a balance between business and pleasure. You should create hours that suit you, and once these become agreeable with your schedule, you should share them with your family–it is important that they know when you are working and when you are free.

Make sure that you choose office hours when your body is rested and refreshed. You do not want to work when you are fatigued. Working when you are fresh ensures you are productive and can accomplish some of the most demanding tasks. Once you identify appropriate office hours, make sure that you stick to these.

Set Up Business Savings and Checking Accounts

Keep personal and business finances separate. You may need to have both a savings and checking account for business. You also need to think about signing up for third-party payment processors, especially if you will be accepting credit cards or online payments. To choose the best bank account and payment method for your needs, do some research and see what really fits for you.

Get a Postal Address If Necessary

Sometimes you may need a postal address where you will receive all official communications. It's a good idea to have this in mind even if you don't need it all the time. A postal address will get you to stand out as an organized broker and also an organized manager. You may choose to use the postal address for invoices, direct mailings, and company letterheads. This also allows you to keep your home or personal address separate from your business address.
Working from home has numerous advantages. You will have access to a standard office, but without the costs and overheads you would expect from a regular commercial office.

Book Keeping and Accounting

You need to keep in mind that there are backroom issues involving your truck brokering business. These include invoicing, bookkeeping, payables, and invoicing. If you don't have experience in business business and accounting, then you had better fold your sleeves and start learning.

While you do not really have to use accounting software, it makes a lot of sense to use it because it makes things easier. You can organize your finances properly and also manage your firm's accounts a lot better.

If you want to get your accounts managed professionally, then you will need to use accounting software. There are several good ones, however the most popular one is QBS or QuickBooks from Microsoft. QuickBooks is easy to use, readily available, and best suitable for all types of businesses.

When using QuickBooks, you will come across the three main categories:

- Classes
- Charts of Accounts
- Items List

These three main categories constitute the backbone of your freight brokerage business. Classes generate expenses and income. The charts of accounts and items list are very closely related. One points to your source of finances while the other seeks money from your clients. The charts of accounts constitute a collection of categories that inform the government about your sources of finance and how you spent your money. On the other hand, the items list informs clients about exactly what you are billing them for. It indicates the kinds of services that you provide to them. These two items are linked together in your accounts.

Classes inform you how the income was generated. If you are a freight broker, then you would set up your clients as a class. You would want to know how much each of your clients paid you. In the end, the final accounts statement will let you know how much money you made, how much your expenses were, and what your profits margin are.

Invoicing Clients

As a service provider, your clients will be expecting a bill once the service has been satisfactorily delivered. When you invoice your clients, you want to provide them with detailed information about the services provided. For instance, you might charge a client for moving their cargo. Your clients often have a choice of payment methods and will choose one of three methods. These methods include:

- Flat fee payment

- Fee per mile
- Payment by the hundredweight

When invoicing your clients, you will need to spell out the fee payment method. The flat rate method is pretty obvious. You may, for instance, agree to deliver a package for a client to a particular destination at a fixed price.

Sometimes these are not the only charges to the client. Using accounting software such as QuickBooks will help you process all your income, payments, show you what your profits are, what taxes you need to pay, and so on. However, you will need to set it up appropriately before you can begin using it productively.

Many freight brokers know that they will be involved in some form of accounting and bookkeeping at some point in their business. In this case, the chart of accounts is a good point to start with. This chart is essentially a listing of the entire accounting transactions that you might expect to encounter as a freight broker. The list can include some or all of the following:

- Your assets, such as accounts receivable and cash in the bank;
- Liabilities, such as accounts payable and also both income and expenditure are included;
- Income and expenditure, including payments to your shippers and your profits; and
- Expenses, such as loading board fees, office overheads, and telephone costs.

You should assign a certain code or number to each transaction so that it is easy to plug in the figures when doing your accounts. When these figures are entered into your accounting software, you will then receive a financial statement that will let you know about your firm's financial affairs.

Accounting Mistakes to Avoid

While we endeavor to work hard and do the best that we can, freight brokers likely to make expensive errors on occasion. Your job generally keeps you very busy throughout the week, so you might hardly have the time to do much else. Bookkeeping and accounting are core activities that you should do, so it is important that you get organized and undertake these activities well.

Do Not Attempt to Do Everything

Some business owners often try to save money by doing all the core activities themselves. New freight brokers with little accounting knowledge may insist on doing all the accounting themselves or delegate the task to less experienced staff members or even a family member. While this can save you money in the short-term, some costly errors in the future could cost you huge losses. If you are well-established, you should hire a bookkeeper; otherwise, consult an accountant and get everything set up properly.

Stop Postponing Crucial Tasks

Managing a freight broker business is hard work. Many freight brokers are often so busy they forget to perform vital tasks such as bookkeeping. Important bookkeeping tasks such as credit card accounts and reconciling bank statements are crucial and should not be postponed unnecessarily. When you reconcile your bank statements, you receive an accurate picture of your financial position. Postponing such basic bookkeeping tasks can be easy, but the ramifications may hit home one day when you realize that your credit levels are unsustainable. With regular bookkeeping, you will be able to trace any lost checks, missing deposits, or even fraudulent transactions.

Always Track Receivables and Invoices

If you wish to get paid for your hard work, then you should always account for your receivables. Getting paid should be a huge part of your focus, so always focus on doing things that ensure you get paid. Payment means cash for you and your business. Your business needs money to foot bills, pay workers, and even pay transporters.
If you want to avoid delayed payments, then always focus on important matters such as tracking receivables and invoices. And if you should feel short on cash from time to time, then you may want to consider something known as invoice factoring. Invoice factoring is the process of getting your invoices paid by a third party, usually a finance company, for a small fee. This will ensure that you get access to much-needed finances almost instantly.

Don't Ignore Liabilities

Liabilities often constitute the debt and other monies that you owe to others. Whenever you are doing your accounts, always cancel out any liabilities that have been paid. Ensure that they do not remain in the books after clearing pending payments. Should you forget to reverse liabilities after payments are made, then you will have a larger bill of liabilities, and this will give your business a bad name.

Ensure that you can accurately and properly do your bookkeeping. If not, then employ a bookkeeper, so they keep an eye on the finances for you. Also, try to ensure that you have an accounting firm or a CPA look over your accounts from time to time. Do not worry about their fees because this is a sound investment in your business.

Categorize Your Expenses Accurately

Many new and inexperienced truck brokers, or their bookkeepers, often get confused and misplace certain expenses. Expenses should, therefore, be appropriately labeled to avoid any unnecessary confusion. When there are too many categories, it gives the wrong image to lenders and sureties. The general opinion will be that your books are not properly prepared. You should ensure that you set up an accounting system that is easy to use, straightforward, and devoid of errors. Sometimes it is easier to consult a CPA annually to avoid common mistakes like those mentioned.

Ensure Invoices Contain All Essential Details

You must ensure that you provide all the necessary details in the invoices you intend to submit to your clients. There are various details needed based on your clients' preferred billing method. Ensure that you follow the proper invoicing mechanism as required.

Use Accounting Software Functions Appropriately

There are plenty of new business owners, including freight brokers, who invest in top-quality software but do not make use of all the useful features. This is because they never take the chance to learn how to use these features. If you are employed by a bookkeeper or an accountant, then this is probably not necessarily an issue for you.
However, if you are the accountant, then you should take the time to learn how certain accounting software works. The most popular software on the market currently is QuickBooks; it is recommended you learn FMEA all of its useful features. When used correctly, the right accounting software will provide you with a clear and accurate picture of your firm's finances and will also save your money.

Pros and Cons of Factoring Invoices

Companies that face financial challenges due to slow-paying clients often consider an option known as invoice factoring. More specifically, it is a process where a business gets its invoices paid off by another company, usually a third party, at a certain rate.

Businesses use this option when they need funds to offset payments such as office overheads, salaries, and payments to transporters. This situation arises because some clients take too long to pay invoices. Most clients take about a month or longer to pay invoices, while freight brokers pay transporters almost immediately. It is this need for cash that creates a challenge and necessitates invoice factoring.

Pros of Invoice Factoring to Freight Brokers

- Immediate access to finances
- You can pay your carriers
- You get the power to dictate terms to your clients
- You can properly manage credit
- It is an easy way of gaining access to credit
- Invoice factoring provides short-term solutions
- The amount of credit can increase over time
- Your invoices act as collateral
- There is no need to give up any equity
- Even small businesses can access this line of credit

While there are numerous pros or advantages of invoice factoring, there are certain disadvantages. For starters, it does not provide a perfect solution. Here are some cons associated with it:

- It is a very costly line of credit.
- It is a labor-intensive process.
- Invoice factoring solves only a single problem.
- Companies providing the finance will contact your clients.
- Some clients may refuse to honor invoices.

Chapter 8. Legal Requirements: What You Need and How to Get It

Now that you have gained the necessary education and industry experience, you need to move to the next level. The crucial initial steps of setting up your business will involve getting licensed and getting your business registered. To finish these tasks, you will need to fill out some paperwork. The process will include:

- Registering your business with the state government.
- Applying for a license with the federal government.
- Taking out an essential surety bond that covers against unseen hazards.

Fortunately, all these processes can be done and completed online. If you have a credit card, a connected computer, and resources to get a hold of all other required forms and fees, then you will be able to accomplish these crucial, yet straightforward steps within a few minutes.

Federal Licensing Requirements

Any brokers that ship merchandise across state lines need to seek authorization from the federal government. The government's arm for registering freight brokers is the Federal Motor Carrier Safety Administration (FMCSA). When you submit your application forms as well as a small processing fee, you should receive your license within four-six weeks. Before the year 2015, brokers had to fill out a number of forms and then submit them to the FMCSA either via post or email. However, things have changed since then. Make use of the Unified Registration System (URS). The URS puts together all the forms that you need to sign to streamline the application process.

Apply for the Operating Authority

One of the initial steps of seeking federal licensing is the application for the operating authority. This is also referred to as the MC number and simply the authority granted to you by the federal government to work as a freight broker. The federal government has an elaborate Unified Carrier Registration process for freight brokers with agents across different cities or towns. You will need to designate an agent or representative within each state where you operate. The federal government normally issues two types of operating authorities:

- Authority for household goods brokers.
- Authority for property brokers.

To be very sure, you should apply for both types of operating authorities, and the good news is, you are actually allowed to do so. Each cost approximately $300. During the license application process, the federal government will request certain information, such as:

- Personal and contact information.
- Social security number.
- Employer identification number.

Sometimes the government requires you to obtain a USDOT number if you intend to act as a motor carrier. Therefore, it's best to be ready for this step during the licensing process.

Receive a Grant Letter and MC/FF Number

After your application has been both received and processed, you will receive an MC/FF number. This number is also known as your operating authority granted by the federal government. You will need this number most of the time as you execute your duties. However, even at this stage, you won't have completed the entire process just yet.

First, the federal government, through the Department of Transport, will send you a grant letter. You will have to wait ten days, during which anyone could question your application. After that, you can begin the process of applying for surety bonds. Freight brokers often apply for the BMC-84 bond, which is suitable for freight brokers. That's type of financial protection worth $75,000. As a broker, this guarantees your client's compensation—should you fail to adhere to all laws and federal regulations governing cargo handling and transportation. Your clients will be free to file a claim for compensation if your actions cause loss or damages.

As a freight broker, you will obtain bonds through agencies such as Lance Surety Bonds. They often collaborate with bond companies that issue the bonds and then back them with financial muscle. During the bond application process, the bond agency will offer you a quote that refers to the cost at which your bond can be obtained. Certain factors will determine this cost. These include certain financial indicators, such as your personal credit score. The normal rates range from 1-5% of the total bond amount, usually $75,000.

Once your bond application is approved, the bond company then informs the FMCSA. You also will have the ability of entering into a Trust Fund Agreement instead of the surety bond. However, you will have to give the full amount of $75,000 to the fund. Most new brokers find this to be a huge challenge, and it tends to lock up financial resources that could be used in other ways.

When searching for a suitable bond agency to get a bond, make sure that the chosen agency is affiliated with T-listed and A-rated companies. Such companies are considered financially stable, reliable, and will guarantee to stand by you in case one of your clients files a claim.

Apply for Freight Broker Insurance Cover

The freight broker insurance cover is not a mandatory obligation required by law, especially if you intend to operate only as a broker. It is only a requirement for operators who wish to acquire forwarding or carrier authority.

However, while insurance is not a requirement for freight brokers, it is highly recommended. This is because in the course of executing your duties, something may get damaged or lost, and you may be held personally responsible. In such cases, insurance will come in handy. The types of insurance often taken out by truck brokers include liability insurance, property insurance, and cargo insurance. It is especially important to have coverage, since some carriers may not purchase insurance for the cargo they are transporting.

Also, when you eventually employ at least two workers, you will need to acquire workers' compensation insurance. This type of cover is necessary and mandatory for all employers in all states. This is regardless of the type of business that is being undertaken.

Ensure that you confirm with your carriers if they have appropriate insurance cover. There are a number of cases where freight brokers have been sued or pursued workers' compensation, and successfully so, by employees of carrier companies, even when these employees did not work for the brokers. Unless state regulations exempt them from workers' compensation cover, they should have an appropriate cover for their workers.

Ensure That You Designate Process Agents

As soon as you obtain your FF/MC number, you should then designate your process agents. Your agents need to be designated for each state that you plan to open an office or at least where you intend to have contracts. You are allowed to be an agent within your own state where you have your office and are based. If no one protests your application within the designated protest period, and you were able to comply with all the federal government's requirements, then the FCMSA will proceed to issue you with your freight broker license, which will be your operating authority.

If, at this point, you have managed to officially become a licensed freight broker, congratulations!

Chapter 9. Financing and Insurance Coverage

As a freight broker, like most jobs, it is important to understand the risks and liabilities you are required to take on.

Freight brokers are liable for any freight payments that have not been collected by the time of shipment or delivery, as well as any freight loss, damage, or theft claims. The freight broker is required to pay all outstanding balances within a reasonable time frame and should usually be able to recover funds from the freight forwarder, carrier, or shipper.

This liability can be transferred through an insurance policy issued by a third-party insurance broker. The policy will reflect the type of coverage you would like to have in case of loss and accident, which can be property damage or bodily injury. It is important to know that the freight broker may not necessarily have to file a lawsuit to recover the legal fees; policies usually specify that the insurance company will pay for any losses or claims made against your freight broker business.

Freight loss or damage can come in many forms. Cargo can be damaged directly in transit, through improper packaging, or it can be completely lost when shipped through air freight, trucking, or rail. When you are shipping by air, a policy can cover any out-of-pocket expenses you might incur, as well as any penalties and taxes charged by the airline and airport authority if your cargo has been improperly packaged for transport by air.

Freight brokerage policyholders must understand that if claims are made on the policy, they may be responsible for paying a portion of the claims and their deductible. Policies will usually require you to be financially responsible for any losses on your account.

General Liability

General liability is another important type of insurance. This insurance covers your business equipment and other property from risks such as fire, theft, or property damage caused by an employee who works for your freight brokerage business. It also covers any legal fees that might occur in the event of a lawsuit or law enforcement investigation against you as an individual or your freight brokerage business, resulting from a third-party injury claim. General liability is one of the most commonly purchased policies in this industry.

Business Interruption Insurance

Business interruption (BI) insurance is something you should consider purchasing. This pays for a percentage of your freight brokerage business expenses in the event of a shutdown due to property damage, property theft, or even death. This is important to have if you expect a large portion of your income to come from independent sales agents who work for you and your business.

The cost of freight brokerage liability insurance varies depending on the type of insurance and other factors such as the number of offices and employees you have, or whether or not you're in a

hazardous business area. Different carriers offer different types of coverage at varying prices, so it's best to compare several policies before settling on one carrier. General liability insurance on average costs around $3,000 per year. BI and other specialty policies can run you up to $5,000 per year.

Freight brokers should always read the fine print on any insurance policy they purchase to make sure they are always aware of their rights and responsibilities in case of an insurance claim.

Chapter 10. 7 Successful Marketing Ideas to Gain Customers in the Freight Brokerage Business

Once your buyer personas have been figured out and you know your prospect list, it's time to begin marketing yourself to them. Before, however, you must have a professional-looking website up and running. These days, you cannot hope to come across as a serious business partner unless you have some sort of web presence. Thus, it's ideal to have a site and be present on social media.

Your website is digital real estate. Think of it like this: You want to buy something and walk into a store that's dimly lit and is extremely difficult to navigate. Are you likely to visit that store again? You might if it's the only one that sells what you're looking for. However, if another store that's well run opens up nearby, you'll likely visit the newer store for a better experience.

This is how it works with your website as well. Your prospective customers are touring your office to figure out how you run your business. If the website does not appear professional or doesn't communicate professionalism and expertise, you're not going to attract too many customers to your company.

There are many website design platforms available. WordPress is the most popular because it's easy to integrate into everything. However, you'll have to do everything by yourself on WordPress or hire someone to do it for you. Some platforms such as Wix and Squarespace offer a drag-and-drop ability, and they make it extremely simple to design a great website. It's easy to carry out email marketing and integrate other marketing tools using their built-in tools. With WordPress, you'll have to utilize plugins that connect to your website and integrate them. This isn't to say that WordPress is a bad choice; it's just that it isn't a one-stop solution.

It might be worthwhile for you to pay a web designer to create your website if you happen to be particularly bad at it. Some old-school freight brokers have terrible-looking websites, so you might be fooled into thinking that a website isn't really necessary. However, those old companies can survive on their legacy relationships. You don't have that luxury, so invest in your website. It's an asset that you must take full advantage of.

Your website should have the following units at a minimum:

- About us - This is where you talk about your company's niche and specialization. If you can highlight your or your partners' experience, talk about it here.
- Services - You can have this be your homepage. Talk about the services you offer and why you're the best choice for customers in your niche.
- Contact us - Make it extremely easy for people to contact you. Have your phone number in your website header so that it's always present. This page should have a contact form and must also indicate your office address.

- Testimonials - This one will be hard to come by when you're starting out. Ideally, you'll have testimonials from satisfied customers. When you begin, consider using testimonials from your carriers, talking about how professional you are, and explaining how you're the best choice.
- Blog - Your blog is going to be your greatest marketing tool. It's also something that most freight brokers ignore because they're too impatient. Use it well, and you'll manage to truly stand out.

After your website is up and working, you can begin using the different marketing tactics I'm about to detail. Not all of these will work for you. Some might show results quickly, while others will take time to work their magic. It's critical that you maintain your focus and measure which methods are giving you the best ROI.

Some methods, such as blog content marketing, will take time to bear fruit. If you stick with it, you'll manage to build a pipeline that stays full no matter what. Make sure to keep going even if you don't get quick results from them.

Cold Calling/Emails

Using this strategy of freight broker sales has been proven to be successful. Before the internet exploded, it was the only way sales reps from freight brokers could get the attention of prospective customers. Cold calling is a numbers game, and more often than not, you'll struggle to make an impression. However, the more you call, the more likely it is that you'll manage to land someone who can become a great customer.

There are many ways of getting phone numbers you can try. Zoominfo is a great B2B journal that you can subscribe to. They give you access to a database that has listings of 60 million businesses in the United States, and it costs $995 per year. If you land even one customer, the cost of a subscription becomes insignificant.

Other cold calling leads databases include Lead411 and Jigsaw by Salesforce. Lead411 has over 100,000 companies and over 700,000 executives and costs $29.95 per month. Pay $39.95 per month, and you'll get access to three times the number of contacts. Jigsaw costs $250 per year and allows you to upload contacts directly to your CRM database on your website. You can download 350 contacts per month.

You don't have to subscribe to all of these services. Obviously, the more you subscribe to, the greater the number of potential contacts you have. However, subscribing to just one service is enough. Remember that cold calling isn't going to land you a client on the first try. It merely brings them into the fold and allows you to introduce yourself to them. Your objective should be to get an email address at the very least. If you already have this information, you should try to set up an in-person meeting where you can explain your services to them.

Most people won't agree to this and will ask you to send them your marketing material. Therefore, you will need to have brochures ready to go. Your brochure can be a print version of your website, so you don't need to go overboard with it. Set aside sometime every day to cold call potential clients. Consistency is key.

Remember to follow up with your cold calls, too. Note when you called them and follow up with a call the next month. The objective of your entire marketing strategy is to remain at the forefront of their minds. Following up is crucial and how you'll manage to do this. Don't be pushy or push to "close" or anything. Your customers will come to you when they have a need. Use the cold call to introduce yourself and your services.

The cold email is in the same vein as the cold call. The advantage a cold email has is that it's easier to track and automate. You can create a spreadsheet with your contacts' information, upload an email script to it, and have a freelance developer connect the spreadsheet to your email, then automatically send an email. If sounds too complicated, then you can do this manually and keep track of the dates on which you sent your prospects an email.

Your email script can closely adhere to your cold calling script. As with cold calls, remember to follow up via emails. Emails can easily be ignored, so make sure you send a follow-up message every two weeks. This way, you'll manage to let people know you're around in case they need help. If someone does respond, try to move them further along in the buying process by setting up a meeting online or visiting them in their office.

Here is a simple cold calling script you can follow:

1. Introduce yourself - "Hello this is <<name>> from <<company>>. How are you today? << Make an icebreaker by asking for time or some relevant conversation topic>>"
2. Introduce your service - "We're a logistics solutions company operating in <<location>>. I was just wondering if you are the person to talk to if I wanted to save you 10-20% off your current shipping costs?"
3. Do not negotiate on the basis of price despite pitching lower costs. Negotiate on the basis of service provided.
4. Ask them about their shipping methods currently. What are the pain points? What do they want to do better?
5. Explain to them how you can find a solution to their problems. Don't talk about how great you are; rather, tell them how great you are at solving their problems.

You might have to deal with gatekeepers such as secretaries or lower-level employees. Introduce yourself to them and ask for their help. Get them on your side by framing your service as a great thing, but convince them that you can't execute it without their help. This will lower the barrier. You might have to call back a few times to get past them. Make sure you use their name when talking to them.

If your prospect is busy, always ask for a better time to call them back. Verify their information (name, phone number, title, and job function) before hanging up. Always verify their job function since this helps you figure out whether you're talking to the right person or not.

When following up with your prospects, always refer to your preceding call. Here are some examples:

1. Introduce yourself - "Hello <<their name>>, this is <<your name>> from <<company>>. How are you doing today?"

Follow up - "I was calling you back to follow up on our earlier conversation. Is this a good time? / What did you think of the information I supplied you? /Do you have any questions about the material I sent you?"

2. At the end of the call, ask for a commitment. "I appreciate you taking the time to chat with me today. I look forward to working with you in the future. Let me know if I can assist you in any way with transportation arrangements."

If you don't mind being a bit aggressive, you can use the following script. Don't use it on your first call since it might provoke a negative response. Instead, use it on one of your follow-up calls if your prospect isn't willing to commit: "Right now, what can I do to persuade you to accept me as a serious business partner/hire me to solve your transportation needs?" This is a pretty aggressive pitch, so you should use it wisely. Often, a customer won't have a genuine need. However, if it works, it allows you the chance to get to know what their objections are, and you can press your case.

Door-to-Door Sales

It might sound tough to do, but going door to door and visiting companies is a great way of generating leads. It's the physical version of a cold call and can be tough to pull off. You'll need to be mentally strong to make this work for you. You'll be met with a lot of rejection, and you must keep believing that the next call you make will be the one that lands you a great client.

While it's possible to get lucky and visit a client who needs your services, it's more likely that you'll end up talking to someone that will ask for more information. After all, companies aren't going to switch or sign up for new freight providers on the spot. The process takes time, and you'll need to give them space to make their decisions. Again, your objective should be to get at least an email address and phone number before you leave the building. Although it is true that it is not always possible to succeed, always try.

Trade Shows and Conferences

If you've ever wondered why people sign up to talk and attend trade shows, you're about to find out. Networking is the primary reason individuals attend these events. Sure, you might pick up some interesting information here and there, but networking is what really drives interest in these events. This is because it's an easy way to get to know everyone who's involved in a particular industry. You can generate a ton of prospects from a single trade show.

These days, most events are held online, and this does reduce the number of serendipitous meetings that take place. On the other hand, consider this: it's easier than ever to attend an event. Wherever you are in the globe, your niche and product will have an event tied to them. Check trade journals, or simply search for your product name followed by conferences, events, or trade shows. in this way you will be updated on the events that are taking place. Every product or industry has a trade body linked to it, so make sure to check their website. They'll typically have an events calendar. Keeping up with current events can also be accomplished by checking LinkedIn groups for listings. Event sponsors always post information on LinkedIn to generate as much interest as possible.

Speaking of sponsors, if you have the cash, consider sponsoring an event. This is a great way to get your brand out in front of other people. Different events will have varying sponsorship rates, so make sure you check with the organizers. Don't assume the prices will be exorbitant. Some of the rate cards might surprise you. Once you're a sponsor, you can set up your trade booth, which will generate a lot of interest in your services. At online events, you can have an electronic trade booth and attach your website's contact form to it to generate leads.

Conferences are a great way to generate warm leads. Following up with them over email or phone is an effective method for building a business relationship.

Content Marketing

This is an area that many freight brokers do not capitalize on, and this is where you can really differentiate yourself. As for the advantages, you can give your prospective customers an impression of expertise, even if you aren't the most experienced. So long as you're able to supply them with value, you'll be doing them a favor, and they'll keep coming back to you. Content marketing can be done in three forms. The first is blog posts. You can write helpful information that pertains to your niche on your blog, and when people search for this information, they'll automatically come to see you as an authority in your niche. In case you're wondering which topics you need to write about, Google gives you all the information you need for free. Start typing a few words into the search bar, and you'll see a number of suggestions pop up.

Look at some of the other results that are displayed, and aim to write content that is more helpful than the top-ranking result. This way, you don't need to reinvent the wheel. Simply make sure you're better than the current best, and Google will reward you.

The second method by which you can conduct content marketing is by writing articles in relevant trade publications. For example, if you're operating in the silicon chip niche, publishing an article that highlights your freight services in the publication is a great way to put yourself out in front of everyone operating in the industry. You'll need to tailor your article to fit the publication's tone of voice and content, of course.

The third way of using content marketing to drive traffic and interest in your business is to create case studies. Case studies are in-depth testimonials. Once you have customers who are satisfied with your services, create a case study, and put it on your blog. Publish it as a PDF file that visitors to your blog can download as well. Case studies are extremely powerful in convincing people to sign up for your services, and you should use them as much as possible. You might be thinking that you're not a writer and thus, all of these methods won't make sense to you. It's possible to work with a freelancer or with a writing service that will produce all the content you need affordably. Sites such as Upwork and Scripted host a number of writers who will turn in decent work for bargain-basement prices. You might have to spruce up their content, but you certainly won't have to write the entire article by yourself.

Many freight brokers don't use this form of marketing, but by simply putting out good content, you'll build a high degree of authority.

Use Social Media

Social media is a great way to find prospective clients. Facebook used to be a hotbed for finding work, but these days, Facebook groups aren't what they used to be. They're extremely useful for finding carriers, though. The best group is the Freight Brokers group, where you can post ads searching for truckers that match your needs.

LinkedIn is perhaps the best tool for finding clients. Start off by creating a nice-looking profile that speaks to your expertise. Joining groups that seek to connect customers with brokers is a great way to network. Republish your blog content on LinkedIn to generate even more interest in your services. LinkedIn is perfectly acceptable as part of that cold emailing or messaging to people. Just don't be pushy and always share something of value.

Email Marketing

All of your preceding efforts lead to this goal. You need to capture as many targeted emails as possible and run newsletters to them once a month or more. Let people know of your services, and over time, you'll find customers coming to you inquiring about your rates. As with content marketing, email marketing takes time. Keep being patient, and you'll find that your efforts will be successful.

Chapter 11. 7 Practical Tips on How to Build a Carrier Base

A Carrier base is important to freight brokerage business because it will serve as the center for your freight brokerage business. You might have heard that a good business is one that is run at a very low cost and still, has maximum profit. Well, that's one of the reasons why you need to build your own carrier base, because it is cheaper. You will not be paying real estate taxes, electricity bills or even other expenses you would have if you decided to rent a place. Aside from that, a carrier base also serves as a safety net for your business in case there are natural disasters in your area. It can accommodate all the people in times of emergency and it will serve as your office. This is why you should look for a location free of natural calamities.

As a carrier base, it is best that you choose a place that is near the main road, so that people can easily locate your business when they need freight broker services from you. Also, it should be near hospitals and fire stations so that there are people who can help in case of emergencies.

Depending from your needs, you may want to have more than one carrier base. Each one will serve as an office for each employee in your business. If you're planning to build more than one carrier base, then make sure that their location is near each other and make sure also that they are accessible to the public.

Here are some tips on how to build a carrier base:

1. Try to find a place that has more than one exit and entrance. If you're building a carrier base with several offices, it is best that it is near different exits. This way, if there are any criminals in the vicinity, they will not be able to get inside your carrier base because they will easily get caught.
2. When you choose a location for your carrier base, make sure that it is near the main road so that people can easily locate it. Make sure also that the location has parking spaces for cars and trucks and has wide roads to accommodate big trucks.
3. Find a place that is near hospitals and fire stations. If there is any emergency, people might need to go to these places. Also, if you're building a carrier base with several offices, they should be near these public facilities. This way, more people in your locality will know where to find your cargo freight brokerage services.
4. When you choose a location for your carrier base, make sure that it is accessible by the public. People should be able to get there in case of emergencies or accidents—this way they will be able to reach the nearest hospital or fire station quickly.

5. When you're choosing a location for your carrier base, make sure that it does not have big structures in the area. For example, buildings or houses. These structures might cause hindrance to people who are driving their vehicles and this will be a risk to them and also your carriers.

6. Find a place that is near establishments such as banks, convenience stores and gas stations. This way, people can easily buy supplies if ever they need them while waiting for their shipments to come. Also, if you're planning on building several offices, there should be some establishment nearby so that your employees will be able to go there in case they need a break from the office.

7. Try to locate your carrier base near a good school. If you're planning on hiring employees, they will need a place to send their kids while they're at work. That is why a good school nearby is an option that you should consider. This way, employees will not have any problems looking for schools for their children.

Chapter 12. The Most Effective Software for Freight Brokerage That Can Increase Productivity Greatly

All of us want to be successful in our work, and we wonder why many freight brokers are not successful. Why? It is because they don't have the most effective software to help them succeed. If you're a freight broker, then how reading the following pages so that you will know what you should do to improve your work? You must consider investing in the good software because it will help you a lot. One of the most important actions to do is to select the best freight brokerage software. The best software is one that will help you in increasing your productivity greatly. You can do your work easily and conveniently if you have the right software. Also, you should choose the software that allows for easier tracking of your shipments and other important information. In the following section, I'm about to show you several good choices of the most effective software for your freight brokerage:

Freightlogic Tracking Software

This software comes with a lot of useful features. It has the ability to a) track broker and supplier spending; b) manage your contacts and create quotes promptly; and c) allow you to access customer information easily. This software's interface has been designed to be easy to use, which allows you to operate it without minimum difficulty.

Fretello

This Freight Broker Software has the best features that are suitable for any broker or shipper who wants to make his or her business more efficient and productive. It is an excellent option because a) you can get access to 24/7 customer support; b) you will be able to send and receive documents easily with this software; and c) you may use features like freight quotes and invoicing.

Shipware Freight Software

One of the better possibilities for those who are looking to make their shipping business more efficient and productive is this program. It was created by brokers who know a thing or two when it comes to freight forwarding. You won't have any problem using this software because it's very user-friendly. It has a great interface that's easy to use, which means that you can send, receive, create, and track documents in just a few clicks. You won't have to spend too much time learning how to use the software because it's very simple. It can increase your productivity significantly.

Freight Pad Freight Forwarding Software

For those who desire to send their goods elsewhere, this is also a wonderful choice. This software allows you to make your business more productive and efficient by giving you access to all of the features that you need for shipping brokerage. You will be able to keep track of your contacts, quotes, inventory, and warehouses easily using this instrument. You can also send and receive documents like bills of lading, air waybills, and invoices very easily with this software.
You should choose either one of the software mentioned above. These freight forwarding software are the most effective because they allow you to be more productive and efficient in your work. You will not regret investing in the best software because it can greatly improve your business!

Chapter 13. The Daily Routine of the Freight Broker in 7 Tasks

How does the day-to-day operations side of freight broker work, and what are the steps within it? There are certain steps in the freight brokerage process that every order follows, no matter the nature of the load or the destination. So, take the time to understand it well.

Order Tender

The first step of the process is the order tender. This is the stage where the customer presents their requirements to you and lists the relevant information. If you have deep customer relationships, they'll usually call you before they issue a tender. Consequently, it will become simpler for you to comprehend what they want from you. In most cases, the customer will send information over, and it will be incomplete. As a freight broker, it is your responsibility to obtain all relevant information.

Pay attention to whether the shipment is a one-time order, regularly scheduled, or a special delivery. All of these conditions play an important role in determining the final rate. If you use a TMS that has a customer portal, they can enter all the information you need online without you having to pick up the phone and call them.

Freight Scheduling

You'll need to take all the information in the tender and enter it into the freight management system, which is a module in your TMS. This module connects truckers to your loads and allows them to bid on them. You can also send the tender to a few trusted carriers who you know are well qualified to carry those loads. Make sure you vet every carrier in your network. At the very least, the carriers must have the following in place:

- The right equipment that is safe and clean;
- A valid license;
- The right degree of insurance and liability coverage;
- Ability to handle the special needs of the cargo;
- A well-maintained trailer that won't introduce contamination to your goods;
- A thorough understanding of the hours and regulations that FMCSA imposes on them.

You can even redirect this tender to a load board and see which trucker picks it up. As I mentioned earlier, load boards are great to get low prices on tenders, but the quality can be suspect. Don't risk your customer relationship for the sake of a low price. Always deliver quality and focus on providing value.

Dispatch

Dispatch is when the order is picked up. The freight broker speaks directly to the driver and verifies all the details of the load. You'll need to check the trailer type, the truck number, trailer number, the driver's contact information, and their current location. You should also communicate all handling requirements and the delivery location.

There are no timelines or templates indicating how quickly loads have to be picked up. I've worked on loads that needed picked up within a few hours and loads that were scheduled a week away. It depends on the complexness of the load and on the nature of the customer. Certain niches require advance preparation time. For example, if you're working in the HAZMAT industry, then it's imperative to prepare beforehand and double-check whether all regulations are being followed. Less critical loads such as household goods can come with little preparation time. This is why it's crucial to have a good carrier network already built so you can quickly pick up and allocate loads.

Loading

The physical process of placing the load onto the trailer is called loading, and it's complete only when all goods have been loaded and the necessary paperwork has been signed. Make sure you receive copies of this paperwork and file them for your records. You'll receive a BOL, or bill of lading. In some cases, however, the trailer will need to be sealed before the BOL is signed. Once this paper has been signed, the carrier accepts full responsibility for the freight.

Before the driver sets off, you should verify the information shown on the BOL to confirm its correct. You should even make sure the right freight has been loaded. With larger customers that have huge warehouses, the prospect of the wrong freight being loaded is a real one. It's best to double-check everything instead of allowing the load to move and having to call it back.

Transit

As the name suggests, transit is when the driver begins moving freight toward the destination. Typically, the carrier will provide you with a GPS feed of the truck that you can track. It's good practice to have regular check-in calls with the driver to make sure everything is going smoothly. This will help you establish a connection with them, and you'll be able to add them to your network for future reference.

Make sure you communicate the progress to your customer during transit. If transit times are short, this won't be an issue, but during long transits, many freight brokers forget to communicate with their customers. This lapse happens because they focus on other loads and forget that the customer doesn't have a full view of their shipment. It's your job to provide them with this. This is why a TMS that integrates the driver's GPS feed is so valuable; it allows you to automate customer communication and frees your time to focus on other loads.

Unloading

Documentation is required after the driver arrives at their destination. As a freight broker, you need to notify the customer in advance of the arrival time since they need to prepare to unload

the freight. Carriers typically work tight schedules, and goods need to be unloaded within a certain timeframe. Otherwise, the driver might charge additional fees, eating into your profit. Once the freight is unloaded, the customer signs the BOL, notes any shortages or damages, and accepts possession of the freight. The time of the unload will be noted on the BOL. Following this, the BOL will be sent to you by the carrier, and you will use this document to prepare your invoice. Each customer has a different invoice process, so you'll need to follow that format before you get paid.

Billing

The carrier will send you their invoice along with relevant documents. Usually, you can pay them back on a credit cycle according to the terms you'll have negotiated. Along with the BOL, the carrier will send you other receipts related to the load, driver work hour receipts, and the rate confirmation paperwork.

Enter all of this information into your TMS so the software can track the payment due dates automatically. You can set up payment alerts so that you can prepare your cash flow in advance. Once you reach a certain size, you'll have to arrange financing to tide over the credit cycle gap I explained earlier in this book.

These are the high-level steps that are involved in the freight brokerage process. The right TMS will help you automate most of these steps, and you'll have to deal with some surprises along the way. For example, you will eventually deal with a load where the customer provides you with the wrong information, and you'll have to reroute your trucker to a new destination. This means renegotiating load rates on the fly with both parties, which can be quite challenging.

When negotiating in such tight circumstances, always play the long-term card. Convince your trucker that despite taking a lower rate this time around, you'll take care of them on the next load. Of course, don't just say these things; follow up on your promises as well. Every step of the way, keep the value delivered and the relationship quality at the forefront of your negotiations. This will help you communicate effectively, and you'll build a great reputation in the industry.

Chapter 14. Most Common Problems in Freight Brokerage and How to Solve Them

Roadside Assistance

Many companies will provide roadside assistance to you as a truck driver. If you have purchased a new truck, often, it will come with a roadside assistance package.

Also, check your insurance policy. You may have lined items that include truck and trailer towing, rental reimbursement, and other coverage. Make sure to inquire about this with your insurance representative.

Breakdowns

First and foremost, do your best to steer your truck and trailer off the main road. If you can find a reliable shoulder, use it, but don't run your truck and trailer into soft dirt or sand. It will only cause more damage. If possible, try to get onto a runaway lane or another stable place and out of the way.

Investigate the problem. If you can fix something without further assistance, do so as quickly and carefully as possible. Before starting any repair, make sure to set out any required road triangles, flares, or other materials to indicate a vehicle's danger off the road.

Make Sure that Any Work You Are Doing Does Not Place You in Danger of Oncoming Traffic

If the work required is beyond what you can fix, call for assistance. If you have a roadside assistance plan (which I highly recommend), contact them, and arrange the payment. Depending on your location, you may be waiting a while, so make yourself comfortable. Be sure to stay hydrated, especially if you have broken down in a remote location or one with hot temperatures.

Stay in your vehicle. You are safer in your car than sitting on the side of the road or examining your truck.

If this is causing a delay in your delivery, then arrange for a pickup from another driver or contact your client.

Accidents

Truck driving has consistently topped the list of some of the deadliest occupations in the United States, but it's not the inherent danger of the job; it's the accidents on the road. In 2015, over 761 truck drivers were killed on the road. Over the preceding five years, trucker fatalities rose steadily by 11 percent.

Experts have said that this increase has been due to rapid delivery, the rise of online shopping, and next-day delivery. Too often, drivers are urged—by companies or themselves—to go after the reward of finishing enough deliveries and lose sight of safety concerns.

- Never leave the scene of an accident. If there is significant damage, call for a police officer to file a report for insurance.
- Always check to ensure the freight has not been damaged, no matter how small or insignificant the accident is. Check all tie-downs and straps and see that it is secure.
- If there is damage to the freight, immediately contact your insurance company. Also, get the client, explain the situation, and ask how they would like to proceed.
- If you are injured, seek medical attention. Make sure you have your emergency contact information on you.

Damaged or Lost Loads

If your load becomes damaged or shifts, pull over immediately. Check for slippage of ropes, straps, or chains. If you are unable to fix the gear, call for assistance. Never drive a trailer where the freight is not correctly strapped into place.

Contact your client about the damage or issues. Be straightforward and honest, but calm and concise. Inquire how the client would like to proceed. They may want the load returned to its point of origin or instruct you to continue the delivery.

If your load falls from the trailer and onto the roadway, stop immediately. Depending on the situation, you may require not only law enforcement assistance in cleaning up the freight, but you may be required to file a police report. Most likely, insurance companies will want the information for any potential investigations. Again, contact your client and apprise them of the situation.

What about the Freight?

You are bonded to deliver the freight to its destination. It is your responsibility; if your truck breaks down, you need to make arrangements to have your trailer picked up by someone and delivered to its destination.

If you can't call a friend, coworker, or fellow hosts who owes you a favor, then you might even have to get on the boards and hire someone else and take a hit.

If you have to leave the freight on the side of the road for any amount of time, make sure it is secure and tarped if possible.

Trailer Sway and Fishtails

Trailer sway can be set off by a large wind gust, icy roads, sudden braking, or even the passing of a large vehicle like an 18-wheeler. If you have incorrect tire pressure in your trailer tires, this can make a bad situation much worse.

Even before you start driving, there are things you can do to lower the possibility of swaying:

- Make sure your tires are properly inflated.
- Always be aware and driving defensively. Be ready for the unexpected.
- Use lower gears going uphill. On the way down, be gentle in using brakes.
- Consider anti-sway devices and hitches.
- Take potential sway-inducing situations such as icy roads, bridges, and wind gusts very carefully.

If sway happens, do not slam on your brakes, or you will begin to fishtail or possibly jackknife if you lose directional control. Reduce your speed gradually and apply the trailer brakes, which will help the situation.

As soon as possible, you must pull over and stop in a safe place on the side of the road and examine the trailer to make sure it was the wind or an environmental issue and not because the trailer is damaged. It is also possible something may have come loose or have been injured in the incident.

Natural Disasters

You may never have to worry about this, but some drivers get caught in earthquakes, tornadoes, fires, and even riots.

The first rule is your life is more valuable than your truck. Even your client would agree that the part you were transporting can be replaced, while your life cannot.

So, if you find yourself in danger, abandon your truck and find safety. There may be times when you can safely lock up your truck and return, while other times will be a race for your life. We have all seen the horrible video of floods or earthquakes where drivers only have moments before their vehicle is washed away or crushed under a falling overpass.

Find safety and do not leave until you know it is safe or are told that it is. Contact your friends and family immediately to let them know you are safe. Then contact your insurance company and your client to update them on the situation. Again, your life and safety are of the utmost importance.

Theft

Prevention will ward off most average thieves. Make sure the cargo is secure and locked if possible. Make sure the doors are closed as well as any lockboxes.

For some reason, some people are against using tarps, but if you use them, they can be a great way to seal in cargo and lessen the temptation for people to mess with it. Looking under a well-strapped tarp is usually a bit more effort than most common thieves or criminals are willing to give.

If you do find that you have been robbed, contact the police, and get a full report. Contact your insurance company. If the theft impacted your client's cargo, contact them, give them a brief assessment of the situation, and confirm that they want to continue the delivery or make other plans.

Your employment contracts are either as an independent contractor or through websites that will have clauses on theft liability. Consult them to know where you stand.

Armed Robbery

Armed robbery has always been a problem for truckers. When they are away from their cab getting fuel or even at a rest stop, they are tired, often a bit distracted, and not paying attention to their surroundings. This is when attacks are most likely to occur. The news is littered with stories of truck drivers being held up at gun or knifepoint for the money they have on them, their truck, or their freight.

Hijacking and cargo theft are real issues as well. According to federal statistics in 2016, over 600 trucks were stolen with over 700 trailers, a steady increase over preceding years. It's estimated that theft and robbery accounted for losses of over 170 million dollars in a year. According to statistics, Los Angeles is the number one location for cargo theft with other high-crime areas, including the New York metro area and the south, primarily Texas, Oklahoma, and Northern Louisiana.

There is a saying, "Cargo at rest in the trucking industry is cargo at risk." Always be aware of your surroundings and that of your rig and trailer. Park in well-lit areas, even if you are only going to be gone for a few minutes. Never forget to keep an eye on your surroundings and the people you're interacting with. Also, never allow someone else to handle or transport your cargo unless you know who they are. If you are highly concerned or in an area that has a high level of robbery or theft, consider a tracking device in your truck and trailer as well as an alarm and recovery system for your vehicle.

Health Issues or Emergencies

Your health insurance must be valid in all areas you will need to travel through during your trip. If your haul takes you across the border to a foreign country for some reason, make sure that your health insurance is valid there. You might need to purchase a temporary rider, which can be purchased online for a few dollars a day.
Keep open communication with people to know who you are dealing with and where you are traveling.

Fatigue

There was a time when truckers wore their exhaustion as a badge of honor. They would gather at the truck stop, swigging coffee and caffeine pills, and laugh about how long it had been since they slept.
Fast forward to today, public awareness, legislation, and a change in self-awareness have changed all of that.
You need to get enough rest, and if you are tired, pull over. Do not use supplements. Never falsify your logbook if you are working more than allowable hours.
You are risking your life and the lives of others: pullover and rest. No load is worth a crash.

DUI

Never consume alcohol before operating any vehicle; let alone your work vehicle. If you are stopped, arrested, and charged with driving under the influence, you are in danger of not only losing your license, but your business, your truck, and possibly your freedom. If you have employees, you need to have the same policy with them. This is a serious matter.
If you or someone from your staff is arrested for driving under the influence and this includes not only medical and recreational marijuana but over-the-counter drugs and painkillers as well, be sure to contact an attorney immediately. As an owner-operator, this is one of the worst things that can happen to you, and you might lose everything. Consult with your attorney about how to progress.

Chapter 15. Main Reasons Why Freight Brokers Go Out of Business and How to Avoid Them

Sometimes we see any freight business unluckily going out of business, even it has been in operation for a long time. If you look at the reasons why they close down their business, you'll see 4 major factors which cause this problem.

Ignorance about Market Study and Competitor's Action

If you want to run a successful freight business, it is important that you make a proper market study for your area and that of your competitors. You cannot build up a good relationship with all customers in the same area if you don't know well about what is going on in the market. A market study will help you know your customers' real needs and how to become their first choice quickly, while competition is also looking after them aggressively.

Ignoring the Competition's Business Strategy and Action

It is a fatal mistake for any freight company not to be aware of their competitors' business model. You must know well each competitor and their strategies so that you can avoid being defeated by them.

Lack of Teamwork Inside the Company

Another reason why many freight companies fail is because of no teamwork inside the company. If there are many problems inside your company, like arguing, immaturity or lack of communication; you may have done all you could to prevent company failure, but still it goes out of business. It means that lack of teamwork inside your company really kills your freight business easily.

Poor Management

Undoubtedly, poor management is the most important reason why your freight business can be closed down even it has been operating for a long time. A good manager should know well how to run his company and resolve all problems which prevent it from growing. If you don't have any knowledge about supply chain management, there are many advisors who can help you out to manage your company and make it run profitably.

What are the reasons behind this?

Some people really think that the freight business is easy because it only requires driving and receiving goods from one location to another without any difficult task. However, earning a reasonable profit for a freight business company is not easy at all.
Firstly, running a freight company is not that simple as it seems. As you know, market competition has been getting severer and severer day by day and it becomes more difficult to survive in the
fierce competition. In some cases, even though they have been operating for a long time, still some freight business companies have to close down because they cannot confirm their transport cost before they receive any order. In that situation, they are in disadvantage against their competitors in the same area. Secondly, if you want to run a successful freight company, it is very important that each employee inside your company must be professional enough to do his job well. An employee must know how to deal with customers, how to drive a truck, and how to manage their documents correctly. If your employee lacks any of these skills, you will have some problems for sure.

How to Avoid Your Freight Brokerage Business Going Out of Business?

To follow, a couple of things that you should pay more attention to, as a manager, in order to avoid your company going out of business. First of all, you should have a market study for both your own area and your competitors' areas. This will help you know which area is more profitable so that you can focus more on this area for a period. Next, prepare your business plan and strategic plan for the coming year. A market study will help you to know about what is going on in each part of your business so that you can improve it in order to make it much better than the earlier year. Finally, if there are any problems inside your company, solve them immediately. Don't think they are small problems because they don't need to be fixed now; otherwise, they will become bigger problems later.

Chapter 16. Insider's Tips for Running a Successful Freight Brokerage Business

As you set up your freight brokerage business, you should know if you are doing much better than your peers in other industries, such as the property sector. If you can come up with innovative ways of doing business, then you are likely to gain an edge over both your rivals and the industry in general. If you want to be successful, think about putting any or all of the following suggestions into practice.

Make Use of Smartphones

Smartphones have become very popular with people around the globe. They have become even more popular because of apps, or application programs. These apps are an excellent and invaluable source of information that you can use for business analysis purposes. Think about apps such as GPS tracking, confirmation, and even delivery apps. While they are definitely useful, think about other apps which are even better for your business. For instance, apps that help you manage fuel efficiency are very useful. There are plenty of valuable logistics apps that you can use, so find which ones you need and make use of them.

Make Use of Freight Management Software

Smartphones and all the mobile application programs are great for certain applications. However, they are not ideal for all functions. There are certain situations that proper software will provide you much better and more reliable results. Freight management software provides you with functional and in-depth management solutions. Many of them remove any manual processes and help to manage multiple shipments all at the same time. The main aim of these software programs is to enable you to optimize your business and speed up processes for increased efficiency. You can use these software programs to produce customized reports that will inform you and your clients at each stage of the process.

Be Conscious and Aware of Your Location

When starting a business, you should have a certain location in mind from the beginning. Therefore, think about the location of your suburb, neighborhood, community, and so on. You should think about other counties as well. Think about locating your business in an area with fast growth. Magazines such as *Forbes* have put together a list of some of the fastest-growing U.S. cities. New clients can be found in these locations and also where freight brokerage businesses are likely to thrive.

Become a Proactive Entrepreneur

Since the industry is competitive, don't sit around and wait for a new business to come to you. Instead, be proactive and get out of your comfort zone. Try to cut out an image of yourself as a go-getter. Ensure that you get out there and find the business. You should try to meet shippers, and when you do, let them know how organized, prepared, and committed a broker you are. If you adopt this attitude, you will definitely thrive.
Remember also.to focus on your online profile. You should put up a company website and then possibly come up with a blog at a later date. Blogs are very user-friendly nowadays, and almost anyone can create one. If you become an active blogger, then you will raise your profile, and shippers and others will come to respect you as an industry expert. All this online activity will definitely attract more clients to your business.

Try to Identify a Niche

Conducting appropriate market analysis about the market is important. Research, analyze your data, and then make an informed decision based on your findings. The information, or the conclusion that you come up, with will show you whether you need to make any adjustments. Niche markets can be very lucrative and with limited participants, so try to get into one if you can. Avoid taking the easy way and doing things in a mundane and average manner. Otherwise, you will never see any significant growth or achieve your full potential.

Keep Educating Yourself

It is crucial to keep educating yourself. The Internet is a wonderful thing we have today. It translates to information right at our fingertips. You can also enroll in classes online and find case studies or reports and try to learn from these. They will keep you informed about the most recent developments in the world of logistics and transport and will provide you with numerous growth opportunities.

Think about Your Clients' Needs

Many shoppers often need to know whether you are licensed and bonded. They are very insistent on this fact, so it is important that you are legal with all the requirements. Shippers are also interested in plenty of other things. For instance, they want to know about any cargo insurance policies that you have as well as the efficiency of your billing department. Some of them are even more interested in the details of your business, such as the carriers and transporters that you use and your selection criteria. Even your communication skills need to be up to scratch. If you excel in all these departments, then your brand will be respected, and clients or shippers will prefer your services to others.

Business Development

Always remember to remain innovative. Try to find solutions that your clients need. Successful entrepreneurs are always seeking better solutions not just to beat the competition but also to improve service delivery. Your freight brokerage service could get to an entirely new level with more clients, increased cargo volumes, and even high profitability. Remember, when you are proactive, you will grow and become more successful.

When you get started with your business, you will almost always feel like you never really managed to get everything done that you wished to. Fortunately, when it comes to a freight brokerage business, you will only need to focus on time allotment. Sometimes, your mind will be exploding with several bright ideas that you want to be implemented immediately, however, you may end up spreading yourself too thin, which is never a good thing. There is a great approach that you can use which is known as the 80:20 rule.

The 80:20 rule applied to your business

The 80:20 rule is also widely known as the Pareto principle. This principle simply states that 80% of outcomes will largely rely on only 20% of inputs. This means that about 80% of your income will most likely come from about 20% of your clients. This rule applies in numerous other situations in life. Simply put: 80% of what you can achieve will emanate from only 20% of what you focus your time, energy, and effort on.

To apply this rule to your business, you will need to figure out which aspects of your business can constitute 20% of your precious time to produce 80% of the results that you seek. This is something that you seriously need to consider because it will allow you to focus more on these activities so that you are more productive and can spend more time doing what matters. You will also ensure that you spend far less time on things that do not make you money.

Divide Your Work into Categories

You need to divide tasks into several categories. This way, you will find it easier to figure out where to focus more of your time, effort, resources, and energy. Some of the significant categories include:

- Administrative functions: These functions are essential. They include processing paperwork, sending out emails, and handling human resources issues. If you have to go out and pay office bills or check mail, then you will be carrying out administrative functions of your business.
- Operations: When you spend time managing your clients' needs, including cargo, making related phone calls and follow-ups, then you will be engaging in operations. For instance, getting loads from the system, contacting carriers, engaging with shippers, and even organizing to have cargo picked up are all considered part of company operations. Basically, when you engage in any activity that is directly related to accomplishing your clients' goals to deliver cargo, then you are engaging in operations.
- Sales and Business Development: Sometimes you have to make calls, conduct some research, and even visit a potential client. Other times you will be on the phone with your peers and other industry players hoping to acquire some long-term clients. All these activities can be considered as sales or business development.

20% of Clients Will Generate 80% of Revenue

If things follow the normal curve, then you can expect to generate 80% of your income from only 20% of your customers. This is a principle that has been observed and proven over hundreds of years, so it is better to align your plan with it than to oppose it.

To implement this rule effectively, you should consider applying the RMF rule. Using this rule, you will try to identify which clients have spent the most money on your services, which ones use your services most frequently, and which clients have most recently purchased your services.

Once you can identify these clients, zero in on them, and start focusing most of your time on them. If you prioritize these clients, then you will be building and reinforcing your revenue source. You should also spend some time identifying other customers who showcase similar traits.

Understand Your Clients' Niches

Even after understanding which of your shippers have spent the most money or purchased services most frequently, you should invest your time into understanding other characteristics about your clients. For instance, try to learn more about the kind of industries they operate in, whether their businesses are seasonal or all-year-round. You must also know where they are located within the country and whether they require specialized equipment for their work. If you can figure out most of this information, then you will be able to understand your shippers better, and they will appreciate your efforts.

Access Department of Defense Loads

If you wish to access freight from the Department of Defense, then you should try to contact any carriers already in the system. However, your first step should be to register with FAK and with AA&E. AA&E stands for arms, ammunition, and explosives. Brokers can get onto the list of service providers by getting approval from the Military Surface Deployment and Distribution Command. Once you get approval, then you can easily apply for the numerous loads they have across most of the country.

Chapter 17. How to Handle Tax Issues: 12 Saving Tips Every Freight Broker Should Know

Tax is part of our everyday life. Every business transaction involves taxes, and some of the most common transactions are freight-related transactions.

Taxes can be separated into two categories: direct and indirect taxes. First, direct taxes are imposed directly on individuals (such as personal income tax) or on commerce (sales tax). Indirect taxes, meanwhile, are imposed on the sale, consumption, or purchase of goods and services, which makes them part of the selling price. Examples of indirect taxes are value-added tax (VAT), consumption tax, gross receipts tax, and sales or use tax.

Every country has its own regulations regarding taxation. As a freight broker, you must understand the taxation system of the country where your customer is based. Here we will highlight the most common tax issues that freight brokers need to be aware of.

There are two types of tax that freight brokers should concern themselves with:

- Consumption Tax: VAT, GST (Goods and Services Tax), or RRT (Rebate on Royalty Tax) are examples of consumption taxes. This is a tax paid every time goods are sold and services provision has been made. For example, a fuel surcharge is considered a consumption tax because the shipping service provider must pay it every time fuel is used. The more miles a trucker drives, the higher his consumption tax invoice will be.
- Gross Receipts Tax: GRT is a tax imposed on the company's revenue before deducting expenses. This is also applied to freight brokers. GRT must be paid every quarter, depending on the company's tax authority.

Here are some tips to handle tax issues as a freight broker to be able to save money:

1. Know the taxation system of your customer's country. This is important because many countries have harmonized their consumption taxes. When you are sending a shipment to the UK from the United States, for example, freight brokers are not required to pay VAT or import duty for shipments worth less than £18 and £36 respectively (as of 2013) provided that their customers in the UK have a valid VAT registration number and can supply it to them.
2. Determine which goods will be exempt from tax in your customer's country and offer those goods on your website instead of taxable products.
3. Take advantage of duty drawback programs if you send export shipments outside your home country.
4. Be aware of the exemptions and reductions that your customer's country offers on goods that you will be importing.

5. If you are selling freight to a customer based in your home country, note that you can offer volume discounts for larger shipments, so that customers will buy in bulk, which is advantageous for both parties.

6. When you are purchasing air freight or ocean freight services, make sure to find out how much fuel surcharge will be involved in the invoice so that you can build it into your quote basing it on the number of miles the shipment will cover or the service provider's fuel efficiency.

7. Capitalize on the free trade agreements that your country has with other countries to reduce import duty for shipments from those countries.

8. Take advantage of the exemptions and reductions granted by your country's tax authority for qualifying start-ups and small businesses, especially if you are still new in the industry.

9. For those who have their own businesses, capitalize on tax incentives and other benefits offered by local government units when you set up a new enterprise.

10. For those who are employed, consider paying for expenses you incur for business with a personal credit card or even your own personal account. This will allow you to deduct the amount from your income when it comes time for you to pay income taxes.

11. All company costs should be recorded in a ledger for tax purposes.

12. Assuming you've set up shop as a corporation or a limited liability partnership, have an accountant prepare the necessary Tax Returns and Annual Returns required by the tax authority so that you won't get penalties and fines because of late filing.

Appendix: In-Depth Study on Air Freight, Sea Freight, and Rail Freight

Transport by Oceans – Sea Freight

Sea freight is the transportation of goods and equipment from one place to another by sea. It's also known as ocean freight. It's the method of transporting goods, containers, and other materials by cargo ships from the goods' origin to the goods' destination.

Maritime transport is one of the oldest means of transportation. Since ancient times, man has used the seas to move goods for short distances. With the global marketplace and the economies of cheaper production in countries like China and India, it becomes more economical and less expensive to produce labor-intensive products in such countries and ship them worldwide to the consumers.

It is probably the most important means of cargo transportation in today's age. Entire industries have developed to support the massive ocean-going ships carrying goods. This growth has been brought about by standardization and containerization.

Goods were usually shipped as breakbulk cargo, where they were typically piled on the ship. This resulted in significant problems like underutilization of space, loading and unloading problems, unstandardized loads, expensive to ship, etc.

The modern steel container has come into use and is designed as a standard container size, accepted, and adopted by all the world's shipping lines and carriers. The ships are purpose-designed with these standard containers and dimensions in mind. Not just the boats but the transport trucks, the container terminals, the rails, etc., have all been designed to accommodate this standard container size to allow it to be transported anywhere in the world.

The invention of a container with standardized sizes and dimensions in the middle of the 20th century by businessman Malcolm Mclean revolutionized the ocean shipping industry. There is an extensive history behind how the container came about in its current state, beyond this book's scope.

There are major shipping lines and carriers that specialize in the transportation of containers. The biggest of them are Maersk, CMA- CGM, Mediterranean Shipping Company, and some others.

Sea freight keeps feeding the world's demands and needs for internationally produced goods available locally.

Transport by Air – Air Freight

Ever since the first flight in the year 1903 by the Wright brothers, people and companies have been looking for ways to utilize aircraft for moving cargo. The first air freight occurred in the year 1910, when a department store moved a bolt of cloth. Airfreight started slowly but surely developing around the world, transporting goods. The first regularly transported items by airfreight were mail and parcels.

Airfreight started with passenger aircraft. Some of the space on the flights was utilized for cargo. It was only later that dedicated aircraft, known as freighters, were developed to transport cargo only. Airlines found it most profitable to transport passengers on the main deck and loads in the aircraft's belly. Airlines found it very lucrative and profitable. It's estimated that more than 50% of the airfreight moves in this manner.

Airfreight was slower to develop as expected and was a small part of the freight industry. This approach has quite a set of complicated rules and requirements.

Any cargo moved from one place to another by a charter, commercial, or passenger aircraft is considered air freight. It can be one of the quickest modes of transport, but also one of the most expensive. Airfreight charges are usually on a per kilo basis and depend on the cargo's dimensions and volumes. Cargo can also be transported to remote locations by this mode of transport.

Using air freight and other modes of transport like road and rail can result in one of the largest shipping networks. It is one of the most reliable and fast methods of transportation. There are a few options with airfreight:

Next Flight Out or Expedited Cargo

Under this option, cargo is shipped out on the first available flight, which is the most expensive option under air freight.

Consolidated Shipment

Airfreight carriers and providers have flights moving on a set schedule. They accept and consolidate cargo from different shippers and load it together. This allows them to have planned programs. This allows the carriers to sell the freight at a cheaper rate than the shippers. But they will usually wait until they have a set amount of cargo before they ship, which can sometimes lead to delays.

Deferred Cargo

Under this option, the airline loads the cargo on lower propriety once they don't have any other higher-paying shippers and there is space available. This kind of airfreight is often the cheapest and offers maximum savings. However, cargo can be delayed for many days.

Chartered Flights

Air Chartered flights are dedicated flights for transportation based on the requirements of the shipper. The shipper gets exclusive access to the plane to move whatever cargo he may want. This is one of the most expensive options for air freight.

Transport by Road – Road Freight

Road transportation, or sometimes referred to as road haulage, is the transportation of goods from one place to another by road. This could be either national or international. National road freight is when cargo is moved by road within the boundaries of a country. This could be on trucks, pickups, vehicles, etc. International shipment is when the load is carried on trucks from one country to another by road.

Road transportation is one of the most efficient modes of transport when moving cargo overland. It's significant for landlocked countries where there is no access to oceans for sea transport. Zambia, Zimbabwe are some of the landlocked countries and depend on road transport for their trade needs.

Even if cities are based near the port, road transport would be used to move cargo to and from the factories to the port area for further transportation to other places and countries. Thus, road transportation will be an integral part of your logistics and supply chain even though you would be near the port. Even when the cargo is moving by air freight, the shipment would likely be transferred by road to the airport.

Road haulage can also be one of the significant modes of transport for large masses of land, countries like Australia, which is quite large, depend on road transport for their shipping needs. Thus, road transportation could be one of the most important modes of transport.

One of the benefits of road transport is that it can work on a door-to-door basis. Cargo can be collected from the shipper's location and delivered right to the entrance of the consignee. The road transportation industry has higher rates of accidents, dependence on traffic conditions, and fluctuating cost due to variations in fuel costs. There could be other delays due to permits and road rules regarding the number of driving hours, etc.

Demand for road freight transport services can be a leading indicator of a country's economic growth, and it serves as one of the main links in the supply chain.

Parcel and Mail Service

Delivery of parcels and mail service has been in existence since ancient times. Use of animals for transport was widespread, from camels to horses to pigeons, all sort of animals ware used. In Alaska, dog sleds were used, while in Australia, camels were a common option. The invention of the wheel gave way to stagecoaches and animal-drawn carriages. But with the design of the motor, parcel, and mail delivery were radically changed.

Parcels and couriers are usually limited to small packages of documents. The cost of the properties is generally based on per kg. Some of the most significant parcel/courier companies globally are UPS, DHL, TNT, etc.

Today, companies like Amazon have taken package delivery to the next level, from normal to express deliveries, setting the industry standard and raising the customers' expectations.

Transport by Rail – Rail Freight

Rail freight is the use of railroads for moving containers and cargo by trains. This is usually done by freight trains or trains with a combination of passenger cabins and freight cars.

A train with freight cars hauled by an automotive engine on a railway track is called a Freight train or goods train. These freight carts have provisions for loading containers, loose cargo, or even break-bulk cargo. Freight trains are usually specialized trains with purpose-built cars designed to carry loads from one place to another. It usually acts as an intermodal mode of transport and quickly and efficiently reaches the inner regions.

The rules and regulations governing rail freight differ from country to country.

Rail freight can be one of the most efficient modes of transport when measured in terms of energy spent on moving a shipment. It can be incredibly cost-effective when moving bulk cargo like coal, iron ore, etc. over long distances. Rail freight usually connects remote locations where regular service is needed, like mines or processing facilities located far away from major cities.

However, rail freight can require heavy investments for setup and maintenance, since the cost of laying down railway lines, engines, etc., can be quite expensive. It can also lack flexibility compared to the road; in case once the railway tracks are laid down, heavy investments are necessary to expand the rail network.

Rail freight uses many types of goods wagons and freight cars; some of these are:

- Flat cars for heavy or bulky cargo
- Boxed or covered cars for general cargo
- Refrigerated vehicle for shipment, which is perishable.
- Tankers for liquids and gases
- Low loader cars for vehicles
- Open top wagons for bulk material

Each kind of wagon has its advantages concerning cargo handling.

One of the significant disadvantages of rail freight is its inflexibility compared to road transport. It requires heavy investments and a thorough analysis of demand before new rail lines can be developed. The cost is relatively high.

Appendix: Industry Terminology

A huge part of success in any profession is the ability to speak its language. Your clients and suppliers will view you in a new light if you can quickly communicate in the language of the business and solve their issues. The good news is that the freight brokerage business doesn't have all that many terms and jargon for you to pick up. Most of them are associated with the trucking business. Given the close proximity in which you'll be working with them, it's best to familiarize yourself with these terms. Let's look at them in alphabetical order.

Important Terms

- Accessorial charges - These are charges that are levied for performing services beyond normal delivery. For example, inside delivery and storage charges count as accessorial charges.
- Adjustments - Any mismatch between the actual shipment and the bill of lading's description. The carrier often charges extra fees for this.
- Agent - Agents have the authority to conduct business transactions on behalf of another entity, be it a person or company. Their decision-making authority might be complete or partial.
- Axle load - Trucks have a weight limit. The DOT specifies an axle load limit for all trucks to ensure they conform to safety standards. You should check your carrier's axle load limit before confirming any shipment with them.
- Backhaul - This is the return leg of the journey a trucker makes. For example, if their home base is in Florida and they ship to Georgia, the trip from Georgia back to Florida is the backhaul. Truckers are usually willing to lower their rates on the backhaul because they need to return to their homes as quickly as possible.
- Bulk freight - Not all freight can be neatly packed into boxes. Items that are stored in containers or packaging of some kind are called bulk freight.
- Carrier - This blanket term refers to all truckers and shipping providers. For brokers that provide international logistics solutions, a carrier could be an aircraft or a boat.
- Cartage - If cargo is moved within the same city or metro area, it's referred to as cartage.
- Consignee - The entity that receives the shipment is the consignee. The consignor is the entity that ships the freight.
- Consolidation - Combining multiple shipments to save money is an act of consolidation.

- Embargo - Any event that prevents cargo from being handled is an embargo. For example, natural disasters, customs regulations, or government policy can create embargos.
- Exceptions - A problem that is noted upon delivery is referred to as an exception. Exceptions are noted on delivery sheets to record problems with the shipment.
- GVW or gross vehicle weight - The weight of the vehicle plus its cargo is referred to as its GVW.
- Highway trust fund - All highway users allocate money toward this fund. It pays for the Federal Government's maintenance and construction efforts.
- Hub and spoke - In logistics, large terminals connect to smaller terminals that serve smaller areas. This model is called a hub and spoke model. The hub is typically used for freight consolidation.
- Inbound freight - Shipments from a vendor to a storage facility are called inbound freight.
- Interchange of interline - This is a fancy term that indicates the transfer of freight from one carrier to another. For example, some freight brokers organize long-haul shipments through two carriers to minimize backhaul and provide faster service. An interchange of interline takes place at a hub or a spoke where goods are transferred. This is done with the customer's consent, of course.
- Intermodal transportation - Some long-haul shipments need to be transported by more than one method of transport. A truck-rail-truck or rail-truck combination is quite common.
- LTL, or less than truckloads - Any shipment that doesn't utilize the truck's entire cargo storage is an LTL shipment. Not all LTL shipments are bad. Carriers who use the hub and spoke model often transport LTLs to their hub, where freight is consolidated into a full truckload. Some carriers will chart full truckload prices for LTLs.
- Nested - Nested freight occurs when one item can be stored within another. This method of loading saves space and allows truckers to carry more freight. Nested cargo is a huge advantage for freight brokers since they pay full truckloads for cargo that would exceed the space if stored normally.
- Not otherwise indicated (NOI) - A chart that most carriers swear by is the National Motor Freight Traffic Association Chart or NMFC chart. This chart classifies all kinds of freight into classes. The class of freight dictates how it should be transported and stored. Any freight that cannot be found on the NMFC chart is an NOI.
- Tariff - This is the official word for the cost of the shipment as represented in the agreement between the carrier and the broker.
- Through rate - This is the rate that is applicable for the distance between the point of origin and destination.
- Transit time - The length of time that the freight spends in transit.

- Truckload (TL) - A truckload is 23,000 pounds or more that occupies half or more than half of the trailer's capacity.
- Volume rate - LTLs are charged on the basis of volume rates. The entire trailer's rate is prorated over its volume. Depending on how much space the freight occupies, a rate is charged.
- Warehouse/warehousing - A storage facility is called a warehouse. Goods that are being transferred to a warehouse are undergoing warehousing.

Conclusion

Once you have properly educated yourself, whether you took a freight brokerage class or found a mentor, you will want to make sure you have some experience under your belt before applying to an agency. If you know someone who has a brokerage and they are willing to let you work for them, that's great. You would be able to get experience before applying for an agent position with a brokerage. Check if there are any brokerages out there that will let you do an internship just to get the experience that's needed. Most brokerages will want you to have 2-5 years of experience before hiring you and also a book of business. They will want to see what you can bring to the table. You will need to come with shippers already. There are advantages and disadvantages when working under brokerages, whether big or small.

The advantage of working under a big brokerage like Road Runner or LDI is that they are already established for one. Most factoring companies will accept them and shippers. There are some shippers that will want you to have your brokerage established for 2-5 years before they will allow you to broker their freight. Most of the larger brokerages have access to all load boards for posting your freight. Since their name is recognizable, carriers will notice the company faster and trust them when booking a load. The larger brokerages will already have a carrier base established; therefore, most carriers will be set up in their database, and all you would have to do is just create the rate confirmation.

The disadvantages of working for a large brokerage will have you considering working for a smaller brokerage. One disadvantage is with a larger brokerage, they have more agents, so if you have a customer base of, let's say, you and 30 customers decide to work for a larger brokerage, then you may only be able to bring 10 of the 30 customers you had over and broker their freight. When applying to work for a brokerage, they will ask you to submit over a list of customers you have. They will then search their database and see if any other agent has the same customer. If there is already an agent that has the same customer that works with that brokerage, you will not be able to bring that customer over. However, with a smaller brokerage of 2-10 agents, you don't have much competition, and the sky is limitless. You can possibly bring over all your customers. Which for you means more freight, more earning potential.

Whichever option you choose, they may do a background check, and more than likely, you will be a 1099 independent contractor if you are working from home. Most agents start off at 50% commission. Some brokerages offer up to 70%; however, you will need to generate around 100K in sales a month to receive that amount. Last but not least, just do your due diligence on the company you plan to work for. You can find broker agent jobs on all of the job boards and even Craigslist. Good luck on your journey! I hope this book was able to give you a better understanding of becoming a freight broker agent.